Newsday's

Guide
to
The Wines
of
Long Island

Peter M. Gianotti

A Newsday Book

To my wife,
Rita Ciolli,
and lovely vintage years,
past and to come.

Printed in Brentwood, N.Y.
ISBN 1-885134-15-0

Newsday books are available at a special discounts
for sales promotions, premiums, fund-raising or
educational use. For information on bulk purchases,
contact:

Marketing Department
Newsday Inc.
235 Pinelawn Road
Melville, N.Y. 11747-4520

TABLE OF CONTENTS

	Acknowledgements	IV
	Introduction	V
Chapter 1:	**Chateau Potato** *A farming heritage is reshaped*	1
Chapter 2:	**A Harvest of Wineries** *The vineyards one by one*	11
Chapter 3:	**Stalking the Great White** *Chardonnay and beyond*	43
Chapter 4:	**Enjoying the Classic Reds** *Sometimes life is a cabernet*	59
Chapter 5:	**Sweet, Sparkling & More** *A wine for every glass*	77
Chapter 6:	**Vine to Wine** *The process explained*	85
Chapter 7:	**The Match Game** *Which wine with that fish?*	91
Chapter 8:	**Swirl, Sniff, Spit...** *Tasting is detective work*	99
Chapter 9:	**What Are They Talking About?** *A guide to winespeak*	107
Chapter 10:	**What to Buy Now** *The vintages revisited*	115
Getting There:	**Maps of Wine Country** *Directions to the North* *and South Forks*	38 40

ACKNOWLEDGEMENTS

My thanks to Newsday publisher Raymond A. Jansen, editor Anthony Marro, managing editors Charlotte H. Hall and Howard Schneider; Paul Fleishman, vice president/marketing; and assistant managing editor Phyllis Singer, for their support.

I'm grateful to food editor Kari Granville, style editor Barbara Schuler, and many at Newsday for their assistance, especially Alan J. Wax, Jim Stear, Jack Sherman, Bob Newman, Tony Jerome, Bob Eisner, Jack Millrod, Carol Bennett, and Mary Ann Skinner, director of editorial information and technology.

I also thank the winemakers of Long Island, for their cooperation and candor in the reporting of this story.

Credit goes to those tasters who've tried local wines with me, particularly Nicholas Ciolli, Anthony J. Giambalvo, Betty and Jack Maggio, Terry and Jim Bowler, and Cathy and Frank Rinaldi.

Special gratitude to my daughters, Claire and Teresa, who put the bubbles in Champagne; and to my mother, Lillian N. Gianotti, and sister, Margaret E. Gianotti, with whom I have shared my happiest toasts.

And I open a red of depth and elegance in memory of my father, Peter J. Gianotti, who introduced me to Pauillac and Piedmont. A long time ago, returning from the East End, he said "They should grow grapes there."

Illustrations by Bob Newman

INTRODUCTION

This book is a visit to the wine country of Long Island. It also travels from skepticism to belief.

At the suggestion of Robert W. Greene, the long-time Newsday editor, investigative reporter and four-star epicure, I first sampled Long Island wine. Years ago, he had great faith in the fledgling industry. Bob's instincts, of course, were right.

The report that follows is a tour in red and white, still and sparkling, without rosé-colored glasses. Consider it a user's guide to LI wines, whether you choose one from a wine shop, a restaurant's list, or from the winery.

There's current information on each of the wineries to make your visits easier and to help you select what wines to buy. I've listed best buys and highlights. And I've described and reviewed numerous wines.

No one ever should be intimidated by a wine label or by what's in the bottle itself. Wine is a meant to be enjoyed.

So, these pages are a consumer guide covering wines that are available now, some that are scheduled for release soon, and a number of older wines. Since production on Long Island is so limited, a lot of the wines are sure to vanish quickly.

Most of the wines reviewed in this book were tasted twice, at the time of their release and in the last six months. The rest were tasted this year. All the wines reviewed are from the 1990s, largely since 1993. Plenty of the wines, particularly from 1993 and 1995, are recommended.

The book also is meant to be used as a general reference, with chapters devoted to how wine is made, techniques of wine tasting, the best ways to store wine, and what wines pair well with different foods. I've added a glossary to help clarify the babble of wine-speak.

Adjectives aside, early Long Island wines were notable more for their ambition than their taste. They were curiosities. And the first impression from the fruit of the young vines and their rapidly released wines wasn't very good.

But in 1988, the East End had its first memorable vintage. And the mid-1990s, the region has experienced a series of winning years, making the North Fork and the Hamptons a destination for grape nuts as well as vacationers.

Let's go.

Peter M. Gianotti
Long Island, N.Y.
May, 1998

CHAPTER 1

Chateau Potato

A farming heritage is reshaped

I
t all makes perfect sense. Now. A visitor to the North Fork and the South Fork sees vineyards and wineries where potato fields once were planted. New ones seem to sprout with every vintage, speaking the common language of chardonnay and merlot.

The wineries are destinations for tourists and local residents, especially in summer and fall. Tasting rooms often are full. It's as if they've always been there.

But this is a region transformed in a very short time. In Europe, winemakers talk in terms of centuries and many generations. Long Island's life of wine is a single generation. Consider that a bottle of Bordeaux such as Chateau Mouton-Rothschild 1945, available if you can afford it, is more than twice as old as the entire Long Island wine trade.

They have been making wine in France since 600 B.C. France in general and Bordeaux in particular are where grapes reach their zenith.

Alex and Louisa Hargrave, true Francophiles, relished Bordeaux. They wanted to make wine. And they intended to plant the serious grapes: cabernet sauvignon, pinot noir and merlot; chardonnay and

1

riesling. The question was where to do it.

So, in the early 1970s, they drove a Jeep Wagoneer around the country in search of their vineyard. They traveled along the West Coast and through upstate New York, and as far south as Virginia before they reached the North Fork of Long Island.

Washington State and Oregon were deemed too chilly or too wet for some of the grapes they wanted to grow. The celebrated valleys of California were too expensive. At the suggestion of a professor at Cornell

Newsday Photo / Jim Peppler

At the Hargrave Vineyard.

University, who also advised them to skip their beloved grape varieties in favor of sturdier hybrids, they went to Cutchogue.

Cutchogue certainly had the right soil for vegetables, notably potatoes, but cauliflower and asparagus, too. And the growing season there lasted more than 210 days, compared with 165 days in the Finger Lakes.

Farming has been the work of the North Fork – for almost 350 years. And it was possible, if not certain, that this area would be hospitable to the grapes.

On the day before Thanksgiving, 1972, the Hargraves visited the respected John Wickham at his Cutchogue farm. His family had been farming the North Fork for longer than many winemakers had been harvesting grapes in France. Among the comparatively recent additions to Wickham's crops were Mediterranean varieties of grapes.

"He put us in a truck and drove us to the Bay, the Sound, all around," said Louisa Hargrave, a native of Cold Spring Harbor. The granddaughter of Socialist presidential candidate Norman Thomas, she had her vision of the future. The conditions seemed ideal for growing vinifera, the vine species that yields varieties such as cabernet sauvignon and chardonnay.

They saw grapes that were ripening remarkably late in the season, said Alex Hargrave, an expert in Chinese studies from the Finger Lakes wine area upstate. It was as if the couple had "discovered the Garden of Eden," he recalled.

The main "temptations" were the climate and the soil. There was plenty of sun, the most in any part of New York State. And Long Island Sound, Peconic Bay and the Atlantic Ocean gave the land a warm, maritime embrace, keeping temperatures from turning too cold too early. The soil was well-drained, coarse, sandy loam.

But Wickham nevertheless cautioned that "He wouldn't want a young couple to invest everything they had in an agricultural venture," Louisa Hargrave said.

The Hargraves continued their ramble through the area. "One time, we spent a whole day looking at farms, but couldn't see any crops," Mrs. Hargrave said. They inquired what was growing at every location. "The real estate agent finally said, 'Don't ask. All potatoes.'"

But potato farms were going under. Costly spraying was necessary to curb pests, including the devastating golden nematode. Farmers began planting other crops, or simply sold their land to developers for housing and mini-malls.

The Hargraves still thought of Bordeaux. In many ways, the climate of the North Fork seemed like that in the Médoc region of Bordeaux. "We thought, 'This is it,'" Alex Hargrave said.

In January, 1973, they bought a 66-acre farm on Alvah's Lane in Cutchogue. Four months later, they planted the first 17 acres of grapes. And, two years after that, with Hargrave Vineyard's first vintage, Long Island's modern wine industry began.

Welcome to Wine Country

From that potato barn and 17th-Century farmhouse, the wine business has grown dramatically and has altered the image of New York State wine.

3

Many of the early wines from the young vines were considered poor, and dismissed. Much trial-and-error work followed. The wines improved, so did the reviews and, very slowly, public perception of Long Island as a wine region.

Today, more than 20 wineries are in business or under construction. Approximately 1,500 acres are devoted to the vineyards, which produce 200,000 cases of wine each year. Moreover, as the prices of imported wines and wines from California have risen, the cost of Long Island wines has become more palatable to potential buyers than it was earlier.

The growth that followed the Hargraves' effort was triggered in part by the state's Farm Winery Act of 1976 and related bills. The laws contained tax incentives making it economically viable to run a small winery, and permitted wineries to offer tastings and sell directly to consumers, including on Sundays.

Suffolk County boosted the fledgling industry with a farmland preservation program in which the county acquired development rights to farm property. This way, farmers were compensated for the difference between selling the land for farm use and for other development. The first purchase was in 1977.

The program signaled the ongoing transition of the agricultural economy from vegetables to grapes. The potato farms could just as easily have been a real estate developer's delight in the vacationlands of the North Fork and the Hamptons.

Before the new wave of grapevines took root on Long Island, their relatives grew in less likely places along the East Coast. The first American wines probably date to the French Huguenots, who made it with scuppernong grapes in the South in the 1560s. There was wine at Jamestown in 1609 and at Plymouth in 1623. The Virginia assembly tried to spur wine production by offering prizes to colonists.

Imported cuttings of vinifera vines were planted in Virginia in the 17th Century. William Penn planted vinifera in 1683. It's generally accepted that the first grapevines on Long Island's East End were planted in those years, too. There is no record of success in any of these ventures.

But Alex Hargrave found that "William Prince was growing vinifera in Flushing in 1830. He had the first zinfandel catalog before they first 'discovered' zinfandel in California." Grapes were grown on the South Fork around that time, too, though there's no evidence of extraordinary accomplishments in winemaking.

William Prince also introduced the blue Isabella

4

grape from South Carolina in Flushing, in about 1816. But Prince's production was ruined by mildew. Finally, he figured that the region was too humid. Efforts by others to produce vinifera grapes, from Jamaica to Brooklyn, also failed.

"Prince turned north to the Hudson Valley," said Alex Hargrave. "And the wine world went with him."

New York State eventually became the province of

Newsday Photo / Jim Peppler

Wine aging room at the Hargrave Vineyard.

grapes such as concord and pink catawba. Plenty of grapes were destined for jelly, grape juice and the fruit basket rather than the wine bottle.

Early in this century, the state made recommendations about what fruits would grow best here. They used as their source research conducted upstate. The idea was that if the fruits could survive the northern chill, they could survive anywhere in New York. Vinifera grapes did poorly in the upstate tests and, accordingly, weren't a recommended crop.

It wasn't until the 1950s that vinifera grapes were produced commercially in New York. Winemaker Charles Fournier of Gold Seal vineyards in the Finger Lakes hired Dr. Konstantin Frank, an expert on the species. Fournier had worked with French hybrids such as seyval blanc and aurora.

Frank, a viticulturalist and enologist from Ukraine, experimented. He planted rootstocks and vinifera varieties upstate. Frank succeeded with riesling and gewürztraminer.

Wickham's Experiment

Around the same time, John Wickham was growing table grapes on the North Fork as part of an experiment in agriculture with Cornell University. Cornell provided the plantings.

The grapes the Hargraves saw growing on Long Island were southern Mediterranean varieties. They believed that if the southern grapes could grow, so could the northern European varieties and that they could produce premium wines.

These days, the Hargrave Vineyard includes cabernet sauvignon, pinot noir, merlot, cabernet franc, chardonnay, sauvignon blanc, and pinot blanc.

"This really is a medium-size family farm," Hargrave said. "You are literally drawing your living from the earth." Into the Hargraves' earth went rootstocks that originated in Napa and Sonoma.

More fields would soon be turned over to grapevines. After the Hargraves, the new decade brought Pindar Vineyards, owned by a doctor from Stony Brook; The Lenz Winery, established by restaurateurs; and The Bridgehampton Winery, founded by an advertising executive. Pindar and Lenz continue. Bridgehampton, on the South Fork, was a casualty.

In the 1980s, two areas of Long Island were recognized as wine-producing regions by the federal government. Each received the legal designation of American Viticultural Area, or AVA, from the Bureau of Alcohol, Tobacco and Firearms, similar to the "appellation" given by the French.

The AVA is defined by boundaries both climatic and geographic. To use the designation on a bottle of wine, 85 per cent of the grapes in that wine must be from the AVA. For a wine to be labelled a varietal, such as cabernet sauvignon or chardonnay, at least 75 per cent of the wine has to be from that grape.

The two AVA designations on Long Island are "North Fork of Long Island," awarded in 1986; and "The Hamptons, Long Island," in 1985.

And they are two distinct growing areas, courtesy of the glacier that carved out Long Island. The North Fork points northeasterly, has a moderate climate, warmer winds and thereby warmer temperatures than the South, plus protection afforded by the waters of Peconic Bay and Long Island Sound. The soil on the North Fork usually has better drainage.

The South Fork, wider, longer and with terrain

different from the North, can be considerably cooler. There's more fog, less sun. The growing season is shorter. That makes it more conducive to white wine grapes, which need less time to ripen. The soil also is heavier, denser and richer; the water table, high.

Most of the wineries are situated on the North Fork, between Aquebogue and Greenport. The biggest concentration is in Cutchogue. There are three wineries on the South Fork, in Water Mill, Sagaponack and Bridgehampton.

Elsewhere on Long Island, Banfi, the major Italian wine importer, has a 55-acre chardonnay vineyard in Old Brookville in Nassau. Grapes grown on the site are made into wine at Chateau Frank, in upstate Hammondsport. Loughlin Vineyards in Sayville has its wine made by Peconic Bay Vineyards in Peconic.

Grape varieties grown on Long Island are led by chardonnay, by far the most planted and the most popular among wine buyers. Other white grapes grown in the region include riesling, sauvignon blanc, pinot blanc, gewürztraminer, and chenin blanc. The red grapes include cabernet sauvignon, merlot, pinot noir and cabernet franc.

Taking LI Seriously

The wines of Long Island are no longer curiosities and souvenirs. More stores sell them. They appear on more wine lists. When the conversation is about wine in New York, Long Island is the main topic. And when the talk is about American wine, Long Island usually pops in after California and the Pacific Northwest.

The results of Long Island winemaking in the past decade have been encouraging. Comparative tastings of wines from Long Island, California and France often have placed the local wines equal to or ahead of the competition.

A Lenz sparkling wine, for example, finished ahead of Veuve Clicquot La Grande Dame, one of the revered Champagnes; and the same winery's barrel-fermented chardonnay tied with a Montrachet from Louis Latour.

Symposia held by Long Island winemakers have put the wines under more scrutiny. The most significant of these events involved participants from Bordeaux. The winemakers discussed similarities and differences between the two areas. The tastings that followed led to many positive reviews. A symposium on merlot had similar results.

The 1988 vintage on Long Island produced excellent wines and focused considerable attention on the region. Since then, many Long Island wineries have collected medals in nationwide competitions. While it's easy to criticize such contests, where the medals accumulate faster than at the Olympics, they are an indicator of local success.

Indeed, the tasting room at Palmer Vineyards keeps a medal count on the wall, from "double-gold" to bronze. The Aquebogue winery's total is in the hundreds. Palmer wines are marketed locally, but in Europe and Asia, too.

Barrel tastings now are annual events. Likewise, take those from the bottle for example, a major event in Manhattan dubbed "Windows on Long Island." The eighth annual tasting, of about 60 Long Island wines from 19 producers, attracted more than 700 participants earlier this year.

Alex and Louisa Hargrave poured three of their wines at the tasting: the 1995 "Lattice Label" Chardonnay and the 1993 "Lattice Label" Merlot, which are the equivalent of reserve wines, and the extraordinary 1995 Pinot Noir "Le Noirien," which takes its title from the ancient name of the great grape of Burgundy.

But the Hargraves now have their minds on different things. Twenty-five years after their pioneering work, they've put their vineyard and winery up for sale. He's working on a monograph in Chinese linguistics, a project he has had under way for eight years in his spare time.

"We're hands-on winemakers and the thought of moving to a 'corporate' form, having someone else run the winery, isn't what we're all about" he said. "We tried working with other winemakers before, and with a general manager, but that's just another layer of people, and we'd still want to make the decisions about the wine."

"In 10 years, we've had five outstanding vintages and some very good ones," Hargrave said, sounding like a proud father. "To have that many in half a decade, or every other year, is a measure of the power of the Long Island growing region."

Vintners are predicting that 1997 may be the best year yet in Long Island's quarter-century of winemaking.   ❦

CHAPTER 2

A Harvest of Wineries

The vineyards one by one

The wineries of Long Island are as different from one another as the wines they produce. While their styles, in design and in the bottle, often vary dramatically, almost all have very good tasting rooms. Several offer worthwhile tours.

Be realistic about how many wineries you plan to visit on a given day. You could see all three South Fork wineries in one day. But the North Fork requires some planning, just to manage your time. Decide whether you want to go on scheduled, guided tours or self-guided tours, and pick the wineries accordingly. Typically, group tours last less than an hour. Self-guided tours, invariably quick, are also good.

At certain wineries, you may make an appointment for a more detailed tour. The lengths of these will vary. Of course, be judicious in the tasting room. Most wines may be sampled free. There usually is a modest charge for a rare or expensive wine.

In most cases, you'll have a range of whites and reds, from the regular bottlings and sometimes the reserves; and perhaps a rosé, blush or dessert wine, from which to choose.

As you would at the dinner table, go from white to red, young to old, dry to sweet. There may be crackers to nibble on and to help clear your palate.

If you intend to sample a lot of wines at several wineries, be sure to make your encounters a swirl-sniff-sample-and-spit affair. Tasting isn't the same as draining the glass. It's wise to do your drinking at home. The wineries offer for sale all the wines they pour.

The tasting rooms are wheelchair accessible and accommodating, but not all are situated next to the parking facilities. You may have to travel a short distance.

Banfi Old Brookville Vineyards

1111 Cedar Swamp Rd.
Old Brookville
516-626-9200 (telephone)
516-626-6282 (fax)

An Elizabethan-style mansion is the headquarters of Banfi Vintners, the major wine importer and producer of the respected Castello Banfi wines in Italy, including the grand Brunello di Montalcino.

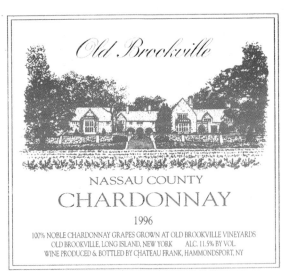

Old Brookville

NASSAU COUNTY
CHARDONNAY
1996

100% NOBLE CHARDONNAY GRAPES GROWN AT OLD BROOKVILLE VINEYARDS
OLD BROOKVILLE, LONG ISLAND, NEW YORK   ALC. 11.5% BY VOL.
WINE PRODUCED & BOTTLED BY CHATEAU FRANK, HAMMONDSPORT, NY

The Old Brookville place is very much an estate.

On this 127-acre property, which had been crop-growing land for Young's Farm Stand, Banfi grows only chardonnay. The vineyard is 55 acres, or at least one acre for each room in the manor house, whose earlier owners included Margaret Emerson, daughter of the inventor of Bromo Seltzer; and Frederick Lundy, the Sheepshead Bay restaurateur.

Old Brookville Chardonnay is vinified at the Chateau Frank winery in Hammondsport, N.Y., in the Finger Lakes region. About 1,200 cases are made annually. Banfi Old Brookville used to make a blanc de blancs sparkling wine, but that has been discontinued.

Old Brookville Vineyards is the sole commercial vineyard in Nassau.

It's closed to the public.

Bedell Cellars

Route 25
Cutchogue
516-734-7537
www.bedellcellars.com

B edell Cellars started in 1980 in potato territory. But Kip Bedell, who ran a fuel-oil company in Nassau County, was making wine in his West Hempstead basement in the 1970s.

13

His first North Fork vintage was in 1985, when Hurricane Gloria whipped across Long Island. The soft-spoken Bedell recalls speeding up that harvest. "We were still learning a lot about the vineyard," he said.

Over the years, Bedell has established himself as among Long Island's premiere merlot producers. His reserve merlots are especially recommended. The 1995 Merlot Reserve is slated for summer release. These are age-worthy wines.

Merlot is planted in one-third of the 30-acre vineyard, and the winery sells more of it than any other varietal or blend. Bedell also grows cabernet sauvignon, chardonnay and smaller plots of cabernet franc, gewürztraminer, riesling and viognier. The newest wine is a red blend called Cupola, made primarily with cabernet sauvignon, plus cabernet franc and merlot. Simpler and satisfactory blends such as Main Road Red, Main Road White and Cygnet are the bargain wines.

Bedell also produces a ripe dessert wine named EIS, and a raspberry wine, which is the basis for a cookbook sold at the winery.

In Bedell's exposed-beam tasting room is stenciled the message: "Wine is proof that God loves us and wants to see us happy." The tasting room is open seven days from 11 a.m. to 5 p.m. There are no winery tours.

Bidwell Vineyards

Route 48
Cutchogue
516-734-5200
1-800-698-9463

Bidwell Vineyards was established in 1982, and its first vintage was in 1986.

It's very much a family operation, with the Bidwell brothers, Bob, Kerry and Jim, running the winery, which was started by their father.

The bright, spacious tasting room, decorated with a poster advertising Armagnac, opened in 1996 and "was built by growing grapes," Bob Bidwell said.

The vineyard is 27 acres, divided among chardonnay, sauvignon blanc, merlot, cabernet sauvignon and white riesling. The winery excels with crisp white wines, particularly sauvignon blanc, which Bidwell has made since 1990.

Some wines are released in two stages. The first, with a spare white label and black type, is an unblended and unfiltered preview, for sale at the winery. The second release, sometimes still unfiltered but occasionally blended, receives the regular label.

These wines are sold primarily at the winery,

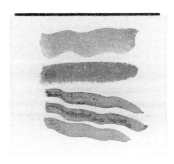

SAUVIGNON BLANC

NORTH FORK OF LONG ISLAND

ALCOHOL 12.5% BY VOLUME

but you also can purchase them at shops on Long Island.

Bidwell's tasting room is open seven days from 11 a.m. to 6 p.m. Tours of the winery are by appointment.

Channing Daughters Winery

1927 Scuttlehole Road
Bridgehampton
516-537-7224

Channing Daughters is the newest winery on the South Fork.

The winery and tasting room, built where an old tractor barn once stood, was expected to be open by

July 4,1998, about 15 years after venture capitalist Walter Channing planted his first grapes in the potato fields.

It's a 20-acre vineyard that winemaker and general manager Larry Perrine figures will grow to 40. Perrine, one of Long Island's senior winemakers whose resume includes Gristina Vineyards, plans to specialize in fresh, lighter white wines similar to those of northern Italy. The vineyard includes pinot grigio, Tocai Friuliano and pinot blanc, and the early-ripening red-wine grape dolcetto.

The winery's first releases were a chardonnay from grapes selected by Perrine and made at Peconic Bay Vineyards, and a merlot made by Eric Fry at The Lenz Winery. A sauvignon blanc and a dry riesling, made with grapes from North Fork vineyards, are slated for release this summer under the Channing Perrine label

Channing, whose large wooden sculptures from tree stumps rise from the vineyard and are reproduced on the Channing Daughters label, named the winery for his four children.

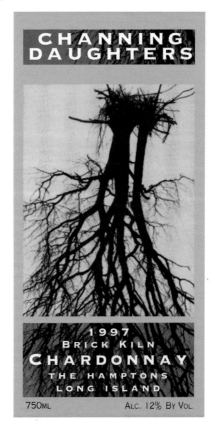

Corey Creek Vineyards

Route 25
Southold
516-765-4168
www.liwines.com/coreycreek

Joel Lauber ran an advertising agency in
Manhattan. He sold it and consulted for a while.
And he enjoyed living on the North Fork, where he
and his wife Peggy had a residence. But Lauber figured he had decades ahead as well as behind him. A
winery had three-way appeal: the wine business was
substantial, the local government was favorably dis-
posed to it, and it was a good alternative to making
a living in marketing on the North Fork. The
Laubers bought land and sold wine grapes

They found the grapes so good they decided to

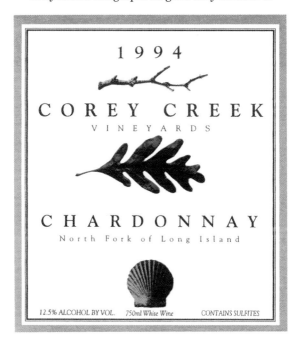

make wine themselves. Their early wines, from
1993, were immediate successes. Corey Creek's
chardonnays were made at Palmer Vineyards and
the merlots made at Pellegrini Vineyards.

The 1997 rosé, blended at Pellegrini, is a distinctively dry evocation of Tavel, in the southern
Rhône; the 1996, was sweeter but equally recommended.

Lauber expects to produce a cabernet franc from

the 1997 vintage, considering it a neat fit between
cabernet sauvignon and merlot. Corey Creek covers
30 acres. Pinot noir and gewürztraminer are among
the plantings.

The tasting room at Corey Creek is a spacious
one, positioned above the vineyards. It's open seven
days from 11 a.m. to 6 p.m. There are no winery
tours.

Duck Walk Vineyards

Montauk Highway (Route 27)
Water Mill
516-726-7555

Duck Walk Vineyards is the offspring of Pindar
Vineyards, both owned by Dr. Herodotus
Damianos.

The physician established Duck Walk in 1994,
acquiring what had been the Le Rêve winery, which
folded, and became the bank-run Southampton winery. You can't miss the place, which was designed to
resemble a Norman chateau.

Duck Walk is 36 acres. The winery also has 46
acres in Mattituck on the North Fork and has made
wine from that yield. On the South Fork, Duck
Walk's plantings include pinot gris, pinot meunier
and muscat.

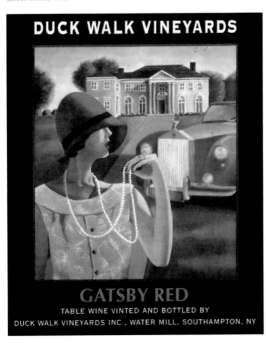

Mark Friszolowski is winemaker at Duck Walk and at Pindar. The Duck Walk repertoire includes several well-priced light and medium-bodied blends, red and white; chardonnay, merlot, cabernet sauvignon and that rare pinot meunier.

In addition, Duck Walk makes a dessert wine, Aphrodite, with gewürztraminer. Two newcomers to the winery are a boysenberry dessert wine and a blueberry Port, made with wild Maine blueberries.

The tasting room at Duck Walk is open seven days from 11 a.m. to 6 p.m. Tours of the winery are scheduled for noon, 2 p.m. and 4 p.m. weekdays and noon, 2 p.m., 3 p.m. and 4:30 p.m. on the weekend.

Gristina Vineyards

Route 25
Cutchogue
516-734-7089

Gristina Vineyards began in 1983, established by Westchester physician Jerry Gristina. The avid wine collector, who favored Bordeaux and Burgundy, planned to produce cabernet sauvignon, merlot, pinot noir and chardonnay.

The vineyard now is 28 acres, with those varieties all represented, as well as cabernet franc. And three generations of Gristinas have been at work

among the grapes. Jerry's son, Peter, is the hands-on manager.

The top wines carry the "Andy's Field" designation, which refers to an eight-acre, gravelly and sandy bloc where the vineyard's finest grapes grow. And to Andy Criscoulo, Peter's grandfather. The grapes that grow there are hand-picked.

Originally, the vineyard sold its fruit. Gristina released its first vintage in 1988, and the winery's cabernet sauvignon from that year remains a benchmark, still drinking very well. The chardonnay from that year also was well-received. Wines of the '93 and '95 vintages are made to last years more. The current winemaker is Adam Suprenant.

The winery's attractive tasting and reception room is an airy, comfortable spot overlooking the vineyard and farther in from Main Road/Route 25 than most others. The tasting room is open seven days, from 11 a.m. to 5 p.m. Tours of the winery are by appointment.

Hargrave Vineyard

Route 48
Cutchogue
516-734-5111

The lattice-label sign outside the Hargrave Vineyard says "1973." This is the first winery on Long Island.

Twenty-five years and many vintage wines later,

and even though their vineyard is for sale, Alex and Louisa Hargrave continue to work their 30 acres, producing chardonnay and merlot, pinot blanc and pinot noir, sauvignon blanc, cabernet franc, and cabernet sauvignon.

While these elegant varietals are the core of the Hargrave repertoire, the winemakers also produce nonvintage wines such as Dune Blush and Dune Blanc, and Chardonette, a crisp and fruity chardonnay that's a terrific buy.

The Hargraves' wines have a French accent. In addition to their current releases, Hargrave Vineyard has a series of older wines that you also may buy at the winery. These wines, including many of the Hargraves' best, are hard to find anywhere else. One of the older wines may be available for tastings on the weekend. Hargrave Vineyard's top wines are identified with a lattice label.

The tasting area is to the right of the entrance, where purchases may be made. To the left is a handsome room illuminated by a stained-glass window with the image of Millet's "The Sower." Group tastings are held there.

The tasting room is open seven days, from 11 a.m. to 5 p.m. Tours of the winery are by appointment.

Jamesport Vineyards

Route 25
Jamesport
516-722-5256

Jamesport Vineyards is maturing in its second life.

The winery was rescued by Ron Goerler Sr., a Syosset businessman whose family has long operated a brass and plumbing supply company. It's in the middle of a new phase now.

Goerler acquired the bankrupt vineyard in 1988. He already owned acreage in Cutchogue, which produces the grapes from which the winery's Cox Lane chardonnay is made. The new Jamesport was born of the two locations.

Jamesport makes chardonnays, riesling, cabernet sauvignon, cabernet franc, sparkling wine, dessert wine; red, white and rosé blends; and sauvignon blanc, which appears to be the grape of the future at the winery.

Winemaker Sean Capiaux said he expects Jamesport to have a niche in softer, balanced wines, led by sauvignon blanc, chardonnay and cabernet

franc. The winery also has produced a fine late-harvest riesling.

Visitors arrive at a converted barn that has been around for a good deal more than a century. The tasting room is open seven days from 10 a.m. to 5:30 p.m. Tours are informal and upon request.

Laurel Lake Vineyards

Route 25
Laurel
516-298-1420

Mike McGoldrick specialized in commercial real estate development through a business based in Farmingdale. In 1994, he acquired what was the San Andres vineyard in Laurel.

These days, about 13 acres of the property close to the Laurel Lake wetlands are alive with chardonnay. The San Andres vines were planted in 1980.

Currently, Laurel Lake has chardonnay from the 1996, 1995 and 1994 vintages available. They were made by Dan Kleck at Palmer Vineyards from local grapes. Laurel Lake's first cabernet sauvignon was produced by Eric Fry at The Lenz Winery.

Wines from the 1997 vintage are being made by

Laurel Lake's winemaker, Greg Gove. They include a rosé of cabernet sauvignon

The colonial-style winery and tasting room is airy and bright. The tasting room is open seven days from 11 a.m. to 6 p.m. Tours are offered on the hour.

The Lenz Winery

Route 25
Peconic
516-734-6010
www.lenzwine.com

A vintage ad for The Lenz Winery took as its inspiration the famous perspective on New York City that appeared on a cover of The New Yorker.

The foreground is Lenz, then it moves west briskly to the rest of Long Island, Manhattan, Jersey, Napa, the Pacific and Asia. The winery does have a world view, and its wines compete well in blind tastings with the best, red or white.

The Lenz Winery was among Long Island's first four, established in 1979 by restaurateurs Peter and Patricia Lenz. It has been under the ownership of management consultant Peter Carroll for a decade.

Carroll, winemaker Eric Fry, vineyard manager Sam McCullough and marketing director Tom Morgan have transformed Lenz by their scientific viticultural approach to create a singularly French

BARREL FERMENTED

LENZ

GOLD LABEL
CHARDONNAY
NORTH FORK OF LONG ISLAND

1995

style in the wines.

That finesse extends from the chardonnay and merlot to first-rate sparkling wines.

Fry came to Lenz in 1989 and he talks about wine with Burgundian zest, extolling the earthy and the "funky" flavors and aromas. The 60-acre vineyard and winery currently produce two chardonnays, pinot blanc, gewürztraminer, merlot, cabernet sauvignon, pinot noir and the sparklers.

The winery itself is straightforward, even spare in appearance. The tasting room is open seven days, from 10 a.m. to 5 p.m. Informal tours are available, but full tours of the winery are by appointment.

Loughlin Vineyards

South Main Street & Meadowcroft
Sayville
516-589-0027

When Bernard Loughlin came out of the U.S. Army in 1946, he bought 15 acres in Sayville.

Fifteen years ago, Loughlin and his family started planting grapes. They've been making wine for eight. And today, Loughlin Vineyards produces about 800 cases of wine.

"People on the North Fork couldn't believe we could grow grapes on the south side," Loughlin said. "We put in 1,800 plants and kept adding." He sold grapes to the departed Le Rêve winery in Water

Mill and then to Peconic Bay Vineyards.

Loughlin's wines are made at Peconic Bay Vineyards. They're sold primarily in and around Sayville. The vineyard now is about five acres, run by Loughlin and his three daughters. It's planted with chardonnay, riesling and a small amount of cabernet sauvignon.

The vineyard abuts the former estate of John Ellis Roosevelt, cousin of Theodore Roosevelt. It's open for informal tours and tastings on weekends from 11 a.m. to 5 p.m.

Macari Vineyards

150 Bergen Avenue
Mattituck
516-298-0100

Joseph Macari Sr. is in the real estate business, based in Jackson Heights. But he has owned farmland on the North Fork for decades. Now, the Macari property totals 340 acres, making the new winery one of the industry's biggest local landholders.

Macari's father used to make wine and sell it in

Corona. His son, Joseph Jr., is president of the winery.

They've recently released chardonnay, sauvignon blanc, merlot and rosé, and expect to release a limited production of viognier this year. Macari has plantings of semillon and pinot noir, and expects to graft pinot meunier, too.

The winemaker is Gilles Martin, whose experience includes stints at Roederer Estate in California and Delas Freres in France.

Macari Vineyards' main building is an eye-catching structure, blending the post-modern and the

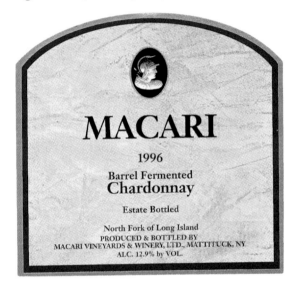

traditional with ease. This had been the site of the defunct Mattituck Hills Winery.

The tasting room is open from 11 a.m. to 5:30 p.m., Thursday to Monday. Tours of the winery are by appointment.

Osprey's Dominion Winery

Route 25
Peconic
516-765-6188
www.ospreysdominion.com

The osprey's dominion is the sky. And on a sunny weekend afternoon, you may see Bill Tyree flying overhead in a classic biplane. He and Bud Koehler are the co-owners, and pilots.

On land, Osprey's Dominion totals 70 acres. The operation started in 1986, selling grapes. Wine production began in 1993.

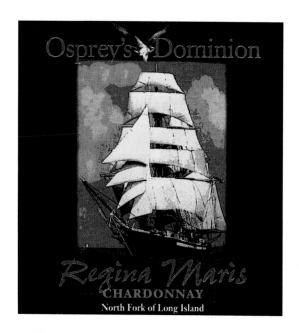

Osprey's Dominion

Regina Maris
CHARDONNAY
North Fork of Long Island

Winemaker Bill Skolnik has an eclectic portfolio. At this winery, your choices will range from varieties of chardonnay to merlot and cabernet sauvignon, through Port, a spiced wine and a very popular strawberry wine. Peach and cherry are available, too. They're fun.

Among the winery's special bottlings is the Regina Maris Chardonnay. It's named for the tall ship on view in Greenport. A percentage of the sales of this wine goes toward the restoration of the grand vessel.

Currently, Skolnik's top white is the 1996 Reserve Chardonnay. The 1996 Pinot Noir is a distinctive red. Some reds can be rustic. Those fruit wines have their fans, especially around dessert time.

The tasting room at Osprey's Dominion is open daily from 11 a.m. to 6 p.m. There's outdoor seating. Tours are available on request.

Palmer Vineyards

Sound Avenue
Aquebogue
516-722-9463
www.palmervineyards.com

Palmer Vineyards is Long Island's internationalist winery.

You can sample a Palmer wine whether in a Westin Hotel, at Disney World, or in Las Vegas. The wines are sold in Canada, the United Kingdom, Switzerland and Scandinavia.

And, if you're in China, you may recognize the name there. Robert Palmer is an advertising executive and he has marketed well, giving Palmer one of the higher profiles among East End wineries. Winemaker Dan Kleck has made remarkably consistent and varied wines for the label.

The vineyard started in 1986, in what had been a field of potatoes, pumpkins and corn. And the winery building keeps that country character, similar to the original barn.

Palmer Vineyards covers 125 acres, with plantings including chardonnay, merlot, cabernet sauvi-

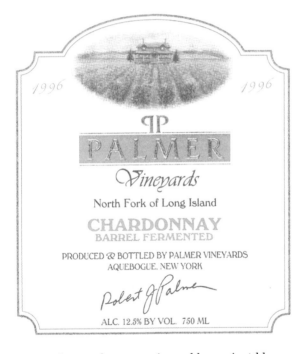

1996   *1996*

ℙℙ
PALMER
Vineyards

North Fork of Long Island

CHARDONNAY
BARREL FERMENTED

PRODUCED & BOTTLED BY PALMER VINEYARDS
AQUEBOGUE, NEW YORK

Robert J Palmer

ALC. 12.5% BY VOL. 750 ML

gnon, cabernet franc, sauvignon blanc, pinot blanc and gewürztraminer.

Palmer Vineyards is best-known for its full, buttery, rich barrel-fermented chardonnay. The tank-fermented estate chardonnay is crisper and fruitier upfront, with a bright, California style. Kleck has made impressive late-harvest gewürztraminer as well.

The winery's tasting room, which looks as much like an English pub as it does a font for wine, is open daily from 11 a.m. to 5 p.m. Tours of the winemaking area are self-guided.

Paumanok Vineyards

Route 25
Aquebogue
516-722-8800 (telephone)
516-722-5110 (fax)

Charles Massoud grew up in Lebanon and studied economics in France and at Wharton. His family was in the hotel and restaurant business. Ursula Massoud's family still has vineyards of riesling and sylvaner in Germany.

He was a marketing specialist at IBM for 22 years. Working in Kuwait, where alcohol isn't welcome, he of necessity made his own wine. The first, in 1972, was a rosé enjoyed in the expatriate community. Of course, it was dry.

The Massouds have been at work in Aquebogue, on what was a potato farm, since 1983. In many ways, theirs is a European-style operation, from the way the vines are planted to the flavors of the wines themselves.

In the mid-'90s, they've made a series of memorable wines, particularly reds and dessert wines.

Their home is across from the winery and tasting room. From the tasting room, you look onto the vineyards, where cabernet sauvignon, merlot, caber-

net franc, chardonnay, riesling, sauvignon blanc and the area's lone vines of chenin blanc are planted. Paumanok Vineyards is 52 acres, which currently translates into about 4,000 cases of wine each year.

Informal tours are available on request on weekends from Memorial Day through Labor Day. Call in advance to arrange for weekday tours.

Peconic Bay Vineyards

Route 25
Cutchogue
516-734-7361
www.liwines.peconicbay.com

Ray Blum, a former air-traffic controller at MacArthur Airport, landed in what would become his vineyard in 1980.

Initially, Peconic Bay sold its grapes. Its first vintage was in 1984, made at The Lenz Winery. Winemaking commenced on the premises five years later. Peconic Bay's wines are fairly priced and good sippers, but go well beyond that. The 65-acre vineyard is planted with chardonnay, riesling, merlot and cabernet sauvignon. Blum, who has degrees in horticulture and business administration, retired from his skyward post in 1994. He's the winemaker. In his office is a sticker advising "Conserve Water Drink Wine."

Blum's wines are highlighted by the 1995 Epic Acre Merlot, a superior red made from a bloc that you'll see from the tasting room; and the full-bodied 1995 Sandy Hill Chardonnay. Peconic Bay also makes a consistently enjoyable white riesling.

The winery produces about 5,000 cases annually.

The tasting room at Peconic Bay Vineyards is open from 11 a.m. to 5 p.m. weekdays and to 6 p.m. on weekends. Tours are by appointment.

Pellegrini Vineyards

Route 25
Cutchogue
516-734-4111
516-734-4159 (fax)
www.pellegrinivineyards.com

Bob Pellegrini is a corporate designer, and his winery has a distinctive image. It's a striking, three-building arrangement around a courtyard that evokes a modern view of the North Fork. You'll never mistake it for a potato barn.

Pellegrini first got involved in the wine trade on the North Fork in 1983. He purchased what had been Island Vineyards in 1991. The first Pelligrini vintage was in 1992. The string of successes is impressive by any standard.

The winery grows cabernet sauvignon, merlot, cabernet franc, chardonnay and gewürztraminer. Winemaker Russell Hearn specializes in rich Bordeaux-style reds, and full-bodied chardonnay. Outstanding wines.

The Vintner's Pride label denotes the top varietals. The red blend Encore, a superior local example of the Bordeaux approach, and the dessert wine Finale also highlight the portfolio.

The handsome winery's architecture offers a contrast between the contemporary and the traditional. It's a very pretty site, too, whether your perspective

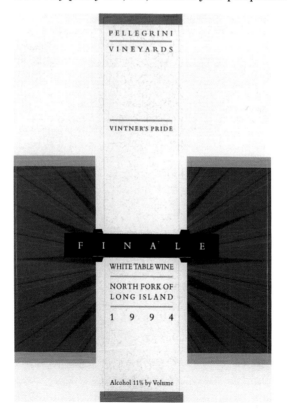

is from the gazebo in the vineyard of the courtyard itself.

Pellegrini Vineyards is open 11 a.m. to 5 p.m. every day. Tours are self-guided. Guided tours for groups must be scheduled in advance.

Pindar Vineyards

Route 25
Peconic
516-734-6200

Pindar Vineyards is one of Long Island's early wineries and it's definitely the biggest: 80,000 cases, 350 acres.

Pindar is owned by Dr. Herodotus Damianos, who also runs Duck Walk Vineyards. The doctor's vigorous approach, from production to marketing, is different from most of the other Long Island wineries. Pindar is no boutique.

It is a very user-friendly winery, with a portfolio from winemaker Mark Friszolowski that's the most diverse in the region. Fifteen varieties of grapes are planted.

Basically, Pindar has taken a split-level approach, with wines going from uncomplicated and inexpensive blends such as Winter White and Sweet Scarlett, to dependable varietals, sparkling wines,

and the rich Bordeaux-style blend, Mythology.

By the sheer volume of the winery, Pindar's impact on the local industry is potent: Damianos has gotten a lot of people to sample Long Island wines, and an extraordinarily broad range of them, too.

The first Pindar vines were planted in 1979. The initial wines were made in 1983. Since the mid-1980s, enologist Dimitri Tchelistcheff, son of legendary Beaulieu Vineyard winemaker Andre Tchelistcheff, has been a consultant for Pindar.

The tasting room, in a century-old barn, is open from 11 a.m. to 6 p.m. Tours of the winery are at noon, 2 p.m. and 4 p.m.

Pugliese Vineyards

Route 25
Cutchogue
516-734-4057

Pugliese Vineyards is a small, family-run winery, full of concentrated wines, sparklers and heart.

Ralph and Pat Pugliese started their winery in 1980. He led a plasterers' union. His family produced wine in Italy, and he started making it in Brooklyn. Their Cutchogue vineyard is 36 acres.

Pugliese grows chardonnay, merlot, cabernet sauvignon, and Long Island's little stretch of zinfan-

1995
Pugliese Vineyards Champagne
Sparkling Merlot
NORTH FORK OF LONG ISLAND
GROWN, PRODUCED AND BOTTLED BY
PUGLIESE VINEYARDS, INC.
CUTCHOGUE, LONG ISLAND, NEW YORK
ALC. 11.5% BY VOLUME CONTAINS SULFITES
750 mL

del. Son Peter Pugliese, the winemaker, creates reds that are sturdy and chardonnays that are fruity.

But sparkling wines, dessert wines and local Ports also define the winery, where trying something new reflects the overall approach. Pugliese is best with bubbles. But the image still is countrified and fun, from the ducks drifting by on the nearby pond to the old gas pump in front of the building. Pugliese is devoid of pretense. The wines reflect that.

In the tasting room, you may see Pat Pugliese deftly decorating and personalizing wine bottles by hand.

The tasting room is open from 10:30 a.m. to 6 p.m. on weekends, to 5 p.m. weekdays. There are no tours.

Schneider Vineyards

Box 1152
Cutchogue
516-734-2699
www.schneidervineyards.com

This is perhaps Long Island's most unusual wine operation. Schneider Vineyards has no actual vineyard and no winery.

CABERNET

FRANC

SCHNEIDER

1994

NORTH FORK OF LONG ISLAND
ALC. 12.5 PERCENT BY VOLUME

Owners Bruce and Christiane Baker Schneider are vintners, starting their work in 1994. He's from the third generation in a family of wine importers, and had worked in vineyards in Burgundy. The couple had considered beginning their venture in

Europe or in California before coming to Long Island in 1992.

They select old-vine grapes from North Fork producers. Kip Bedell of Bedell Cellars in Cutchogue makes the wines. Two vintages of cabernet franc and one of merlot have appeared under the Schneider label so far. They are available in wine shops and by mail.

The Schneiders plan to purchase farmland and plant their first acreage next year.

Ternhaven Cellars

331 Front Street
Greenport
516-477-8737

Harold W. Watts taught public policy at Columbia University for 22 years. He also was making wine in his apartment.

Watts came to New York in 1976 from the University of Wisconsin. En route, he saw wines being made in the middle of Pennsylvania. Watts began making wine at his home a decade later. First, he purchased grapes for that wine. Then, he grew them in Cutchogue. "I grew up on a farm in

Oregon," Watts said.

He's the Ternhaven winemaker and, with Carole Donlin, co-owner of Long Island's easternmost winery. The winery and tasting room opened in spring. Their Cutchogue vineyard is about five acres, begun in 1994. Ternhaven's aim is to make Bordeaux-style reds. No white wines currently are planned. The production is small, about 500 cases this year, but the goal is about 800 cases. So far, Ternhaven has made merlot, cabernet sauvignon, and a red blend called Claret d'Alvah, named for the road and the British term for Bordeaux. The initial releases were produced by Russell Hearn at Pellegrini Vineyards.

The winery and tasting room are open Friday, Saturday and Sunday from 11 a.m. to 6 p.m. Weekday hours are to be scheduled. You should call ahead. Tours of the winery are available on request.

Wolffer Sagpond Vineyards

139 Sagg Road
Sagaponack
516-537-5106 (telephone)
516-537-5107 (fax)

Whether you see it as a grand Tuscan farmhouse or a sunsplashed, stuccoed villa, the new Wolffer Sagpond Vineyards is the most European and opulent of Long Island's wineries.

The estate is venture capitalist Christian Wolffer's enterprise, established in 1987, on what had been a potato field. Wolffer's property also is home to Sagpond Farms, for horse breeding, schooling, boarding and indoor riding.

Roman Roth has been the winemaker at Sagpond since 1992 and he is making a vivid impression each year with these South Fork wines.

Wolffer

1994
The Hamptons, Long Island
ESTATE SELECTION
CHARDONNAY

ESTATE BOTTLED BY SAGPOND VINEYARDS
SAGAPONACK, NEW YORK, USA • ALC. 13.5% BY VOL. • 750 ML.

The vineyard now is about 50 acres, primarily chardonnay and merlot. The winery also produces sparkling wine and rosé, and has made pinot noir from grapes grown in Manorville.

The wines originally carried the Sagpond label. As of this year, all will be labeled Wolffer wines. You'll enjoy touring the winery, with its French doors, antique wine artifacts, stained glass, and vaulted-ceiling barrel rooms with century old-beams.

The winery is open daily from 11 a.m. to 6 p.m. Formal tours are by appointment.

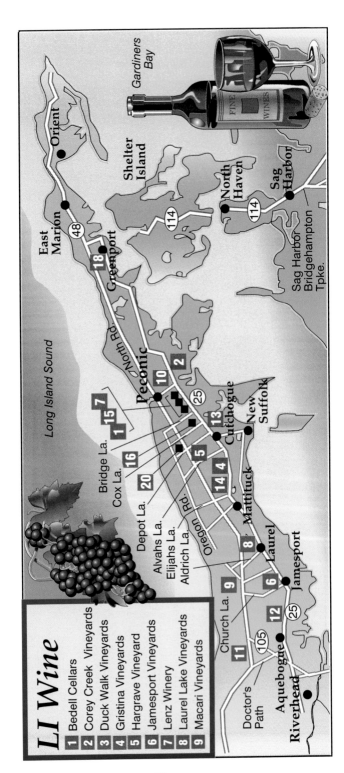

LI Wine

1. Bedell Cellars
2. Corey Creek Vineyards
3. Duck Walk Vineyards
4. Gristina Vineyards
5. Hargrave Vineyard
6. Jamesport Vineyards
7. Lenz Winery
8. Laurel Lake Vineyards
9. Maccari Vineyards

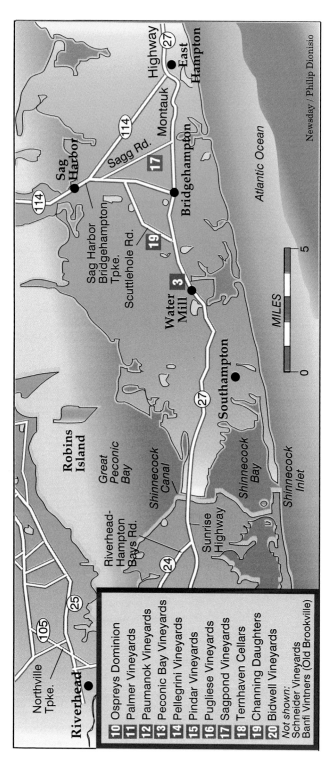

Newsday / Philip Dionisio

10 Ospreys Dominion
11 Palmer Vineyards
12 Paumanok Vineyards
13 Peconic Bay Vineyards
14 Pellegrini Vineyards
15 Pindar Vineyards
16 Pugliese Vineyards
17 Sagpond Vineyards
18 Ternhaven Cellars
19 Channing Daughters
20 Bidwell Vineyards

Not shown:
Schneider Vineyards
Banfi Vintners (Old Brookville)

Directions To East End Wineries

North Fork

Take the Long Island Expressway to exit 73, the last exit. You'll be at the Tanger Outlet Center. Continue east on Route 58, passing the Riverhead traffic circle, until Route 58 becomes Route 25.

Most of the wineries are on Route 25, which also is called Main Road, from Aquebogue east to Greenport.

Paumanok Vineyards, on the north side of Route 25, is followed in sequence by Jamesport Vineyards (north), Pellegrini Vineyards (north), Gristina Vineyards (north), Peconic Bay Vineyards (south), Pugliese Vineyards (north), Bedell Cellars (north), Pindar Vineyards (north), The Lenz Winery (north), Osprey's Dominion Winery (north), Corey Creek Vineyards (south) and Ternhaven Cellars (south).

Wineries such as Macari Vineyards, Hargrave Vineyard and Bidwell Vineyards are on or just off Route 48, which is known as North Road. It runs parallel to Route 25.

Palmer Vineyards, on Sound Avenue, may be reached by heading north on Osborn Avenue until it meets Sound Avenue. Then, go right on Sound Avenue.

South Fork

Take the Long Island Expressway to exit 70. This will put you on County Road 111. Go south on 111 until you reach Montauk Highway/Route 27. Then continue eastbound on Montauk Highway, passing Westhampton Beach and other exits until you get to Southampton.

Duck Walk Vineyards is on the north side of Montauk Highway/Route 27, a short distance from the point where Route 27 splits to go into Water Mill.

Channing Daughters Winery is reached by turning north from Montauk Highway/Route 27 onto Scuttlehole Road as you are leaving Water Mill. Proceed north on Scuttlehole, passing Lumber Lane. The winery will be on the right.

Wolffer Sagpond Vineyards is east of Bridgehampton. Turn north onto Sagg Road from Montauk Highway/Route 27. The winery is about 200 yards away, on the right.

CHAPTER 3

Stalking the Great White

Chardonnay and beyond

White wines range in color from pale straw to deep gold, and in character from steely and dry to honeyed and sweet. Each grape variety yields a very different wine.

Here, we'll look at the main white grape varieties grown on Long Island, and review selected wines made from them. There also is a section devoted to white blends, and to wines made from grapes that are not planted extensively here. The prices mentioned below generally are those at time of release and are subject to change.

White-wine grapes actually are green or yellow, and sometimes shades in between. You can make white wine from red grapes, too. The pigment resides in the skin of the grape, not the juice.

White-wine grapes include chardonnay, riesling, sauvignon blanc, semillon, chenin blanc, gewürztraminer, pinot blanc, muscat and viognier.

Chardonnay

Chardonnay, to many, is synonymous with "a glass of white wine." It leads any discussion of white wine grapes, just as cabernet sauvignon does for reds. Chardonnay has a short growing season and much versatility. The grape is planted around the world, reaching its refined zenith with the luminaries of Burgundy. In California, it's revered. And chardonnay is easily the most popular grape on Long Island. In acreage and sales.

1996 BANFI OLD BROOKVILLE CHARDONNAY
The chardonnay is buttery, balanced, round, harmonious, with a trace of apple, very good with food. $12.

1994 BEDELL CHARDONNAY RESERVE
Creamy and attractive, barrel-fermented and full-bodied. There are suggestions of pear, honey, vanilla, and a bit of butterscotch. A toasty number on a big scale, drinking very well now. $16.

1994 BEDELL CHARDONNAY
To the point, with aspects of tropical fruit and refreshing flavor. Tank-fermented "silver label" chardonnay. Pleasing aroma. Good for sipping or with a light meal. $12.

1993 BEDELL CHARDONNAY RESERVE
A satisfying wine to accompany your lunch or dinner. But its best days will soon be over. $15.

1996 BIDWELL BARREL FERMENTED CHARDONNAY
Tropical flavors and a light touch of oak define this balanced and respectable chardonnay. $15.

1994 BIDWELL BARREL FERMENTED CHARDONNAY
Some pear flavors, a little vanilla, and toastiness are the hallmarks of this rather light chardonnay. $16.

1993 BIDWELL RESERVE CHARDONNAY
Not overly oaky for a barrel-fermented chardonnay, this one also is fairly light and uncomplicated. $15.

1997 CHANNING DAUGHTERS BRICK KILN CHARDONNAY
Very crisp, minerally, and focused, with traces of light oak, it's a satisfying, food-friendly wine. Based on a barrel tasting. Not yet released.

1996 CHANNING DAUGHTERS BRICK KILN CHARDONNAY
The first white released by this new winery is light, a little citric, with some tang. Very refreshing. It was made by Channing Daughters at Peconic Bay Vineyards. $17.

1995 COREY CREEK CHARDONNAY
Elegantly balanced and very good, with the personality of a Chablis. It has mineral notes, and fine acidity. You'll like it

solo or with seafood, veal, chicken. Versatile and vibrant. $14.

1994 COREY CREEK RESERVE CHARDONNAY

A full-bodied, buttery, elegant, appetizing white that has the influence of oak, but doesn't overdo it. Very good fruit and a marvelous, long finish. Made at Palmer Vineyards. $12.

1994 COREY CREEK CHARDONNAY

Smooth, dry, subtle, and very good. It's quite a follow-up to the stellar '93 debut chardonnay, dry and aromatic, ideal with your dinner. Made at Palmer Vineyards. $13.

1995 DUCK WALK CHARDONNAY

Snappy and citrusy, with upfront fruit, and a satisfying finish. Not grand, but tasty. $10.

1994 DUCK WALK CHARDONNAY RESERVE

Respectable chardonnay that lightens up the "reserve" category. Balanced, with tropical fruit notes. Made with North Fork grapes. $13.

1994 DUCK WALK CHARDONNAY

Made from North Fork, South Fork and Old Brookville grapes. Herbal, very modest. $9.

1995 GRISTINA ANDY'S FIELD CHARDONNAY

Outstanding chardonnay from one of the consistently fine producers. This creamy, rich wine is a toasty affair, heady with pear and apple. Elegant all around, with a long finish. $22.

1995 GRISTINA CHARDONNAY

Very good, flavorful chardonnay, with suggestions of spice and pear. Fine varietal character and balance, right for the table. $14.

1994 GRISTINA CHARDONNAY

A buttery, aromatic, medium-bodied food wine of the first order, with fine acidity and a spirited flavor that has an aspect of citrus to it. $14.

1993 GRISTINA ANDY'S FIELD CHARDONNAY

Buttery for sure, with traces of vanilla, pear and some smoky qualities. An excellent wine that's full-bodied and delicate, too. It had depth and the outset and continues to show it. Still drinking well. $19.

1993 GRISTINA CHARDONNAY

The concentrated, slightly citric wine was last tasted earlier this year, and it was holding up nicely. Very satisfying, aromatic, pairs well with seafood. $14.

1996 HARGRAVE CHARDONETTE

True to the vineyard's French affections, this petit chardonnay brings a steely suggestion of Chablis with it. A crisp, light and refreshing wine. More than a simple sipper. $7.

1995 HARGRAVE LATTICE LABEL CHARDONNAY

Excellent chardonnay, plump and toasty with the suggestion of vanilla and pear. All the classic descriptions of fine chardonnay apply to this textbook wine. The real article. $15.

1994 HARGRAVE LATTICE LABEL CHARDONNAY
Very good and flavorful, but not as opulent as the immediately preceding and succeeding wines. $15.

1993 HARGRAVE LATTICE LABEL CHARDONNAY
A superb reserve chardonnay, with depth and finesse, the wine has a delightful aroma and varietal character par excellence. As you'd expect from this Francophile winery, the wine compares seamlessly with Burgundy. Among Hargrave's leading wines. $20.

1993 HARGRAVE CHARDONNAY
More soothing than assertive in its varietal character, this nevertheless is a very good white, made to accompany chicken and seafood. $15.

1995 JAMESPORT COX LANE CHARDONNAY
It has body, acceptable varietal character, and some minerally, citrusy notes. Medium-bodied, tank-fermented, barrel-aged, not too complicated. $13.

1995 JAMESPORT THREE BARREL SELECT CHARDONNAY
Good chardonnay, with ripe flavors and traces of tropical fruit. With a suggestion of Burgundy, it will be fine for a few years. You'll like it with seafood and chicken. $16.

1993 JAMESPORT COX LANE CHARDONNAY
Straightforward, good varietal, but near the end of its life. $13.

1993 JAMESPORT THREE BARREL SELECT CHARDONNAY
The union of fruit and oak is good. But the wine is moving past its prime. $18.

1996 LAUREL LAKE CHARDONNAY
This is a fairly light wine, working as a sipper and as an accompaniment to uncomplicated lunch dishes, sandwiches and salads. Made at Palmer Vineyards. $15.

1995 LAUREL LAKE CHARDONNAY
The best of the first group of white wines from this vineyard. More depth, and tastes fine with a variety of dishes, from chicken to fish. Made at Palmer Vineyards. $15.

1994 LAUREL LAKE CHARDONNAY
The wine was tasted in May, and showed signs of fading by then. Made at Palmer Vineyards. $15.

1995 LENZ BARREL FERMENTED CHARDONNAY
Rich and reliable, as this winery's chardonnays invariably are, and even better because of the remarkable year. Evidence of the winemaker's Francophile style. Reductive, concentrated. Burgundian, yes. But with traces of peach, apricot, some nuttiness. Compare it with a Meursault. The barrel-fermented chardonnays also are known as "gold label." $25.

1995 LENZ VINEYARD SELECTION CHARDONNAY

The lighter chardonnay takes on another dimension from this superior vintage. Fine varietal character, vanilla notes, generous fruit. Clean and harmonious. A bread-and-butter, wine list number, it's a glorious food wine. The vineyard selection chardonnays also are called "white label." $10.

1994 LENZ BARREL FERMENTED CHARDONNAY

If you like a chardonnay that deftly balances its oak and fruit with flair, this is it. The truly Burgundian wine has more complexity than the white label and is comparable to a Meursault. $25.

1994 LENZ VINEYARD SELECTION CHARDONNAY

Refreshing and delightful, this is made for wine restaurant lists as well as your table. Lots of pear, some citrus. Finished with a little pinot blanc. You'll go back to this one many times. $11.

1996 LOUGHLIN CHARDONNAY

Acceptable, easygoing white. $11.

1995 LOUGHLIN CHARDONNAY

Best of the vineyard's recent releases, with satisfactory varietal character. Crisp and good. $11.

1997 MACARI CHARDONNAY

Refreshing, uncomplicated, tank-fermented number from an excellent year. It has the taste of youth. $12.

1996 MACARI BARREL FERMENTED CHARDONNAY

More body in this chardonnay, which has buttery notes and some complexity. $14.

OSPREY'S DOMINION REGINA MARIS CHARDONNAY

Part of the proceeds from the sale of this upfront, non-vintage appley wine go toward restoration of the Regina Maris, the 90-year-old tall ship on display in Greenport harbor. $10.

1996 OSPREY'S DOMINION RESERVE CHARDONNAY

A full-bodied, earthy, flavorful wine, among the richer whites from this growing enterprise. Barrel-fermented in new oak. Smoky, and with some tropical notes and sweetness, too. $20.

1995 OSPREY'S DOMINION CHARDONNAY

Satisfactory in many ways, with ripe tropical fruit and attractive spiciness. $13.

1993 OSPREY'S DOMINION CHARDONNAY

The first one made at the winery, and a good, citrusy starter. Mostly fermented in steel, with some in oak. You taste ripe fruit throughout. $13.

1996 PALMER BARREL FERMENTED CHARDONNAY

It lacks the fullness of the '95, but this is a very refreshing, lemony wine, with light oak and high acidity. $15.

1996 PALMER ESTATE CHARDONNAY

Lively, with lemony flavors and a minerally quality, too.

Very Californian, Central Coast variety, and right year-round. $12.

1995 PALMER BARREL FERMENTED CHARDONNAY

An excellent wine, among those that you'll always associate with this winery. The flavor of pear enlivens the experience and the toasty oak does its job. It's a buttery, first-rate wine with food, especially shellfish and veal. $15.

1995 PALMER ESTATE CHARDONNAY

Fruitier and snappier than the barrel-fermented chardonnay, this production is certain to vanish fast. Very appealing all around, with tropical notes: mango, a hint of pineapple. $10.

1994 PALMER BARREL FERMENTED CHARDONNAY

Yeasty and heady with pear as well as apple, plus some butterscotch in there, too. It's an aromatic and attractive wine that continues to drink very well. Dependable, and comparable to the '93. Smooth flavors. $15.

1994 PALMER ESTATE CHARDONNAY

Another vintage that suggests the taste of California's Central Coast. Starting to fade. $10.

1993 PALMER BARREL FERMENTED CHARDONNAY

A signature wine from the vineyard, the '93 chardonnay has depth and rich varietal character, with butteriness galore. It's still drinking well, if you can find a bottle. $14.

1995 PAUMANOK GRAND VINTAGE CHARDONNAY

One of the top white wines of a great vintage, concentrated and assured. There are hints of tropical fruit in this creamy wine, which is from a single vineyard bloc and made from free-run juice. It was aged in new French oak. The wine has depth, harmony, notes of vanilla, many pleasures. $25.

1995 PAUMANOK CHARDONNAY

Refreshing, upfront fruitiness, and not overly dry, this harmonious barrel-fermented wine is a very smooth and enjoyable white. $15.

1994 PAUMANOK CHARDONNAY

A lean and good wine, with a hint of oak. But moving past its prime. $15.

1995 PECONIC BAY SANDY HILL CHARDONNAY

The top-of-the-line chardonnay from Peconic Bay: rich, mellow and balanced, with excellent varietal character and intimations of melon. There's some oak, but not too much. You can be confident about it. $22.

1995 PECONIC BAY ROLLING RIDGE CHARDONNAY

Barrel-fermented and aged in French oak, it's a light-gold chardonnay with some spine. Toastiness, hints of butterscotch, vanilla, tasty fruit, and very good with food. $19.

1995 PECONIC BAY CHARDONNAY

Fruity, mainly green apple accents boost this crisp and rather light chardonnay. It works as a sipper and with uncomplicated chicken and seafood dishes. $12.

1993 PECONIC BAY CHARDONNAY RESERVE

Oaky, full-bodied. A satisfying wine with food rather than a sipper. $15.

1995 PELLEGRINI VINTNER'S PRIDE CHARDONNAY

A big, creamy, polished chardonnay, loaded with varietal character. The barrel-fermented wine is round, smooth, with aspects of ripe pear, hazelnut, a fine hint of vanilla and a grand finish. For lobster and the like. $22.

1995 PELLEGRINI CHARDONNAY

A crisp and balanced chardonnay, with traces of pear and apple, as well as tropical fruit. The wine is lighter than the producer's Vintner's Pride chardonnays, with much more fruit than oak. Good with chicken and seafood, or solo. $13.

1994 PELLEGRINI VINTNER'S PRIDE CHARDONNAY

The wine spent 18 months in the barrel and does have an undercurrent of oak, as well as fine fruit. It's one of Pellegrini's best chardonnays, with much pear and modest oak. The wine has considerable body and style. And it's made for lobster and veal. $20.

1994 PELLEGRINI CHARDONNAY

Very good, balanced and inviting chardonnay, with an elegant finish. It has tropical fruit notes, and some earthiness and oakiness that add character and depth. $12.

1995 PELLEGRINI EAST END SELECT CHARDONNAY

A light and refreshing chardonnay, with some sweetness. For summertime sipping. $11.

1994 PELLEGRINI EAST END SELECT CHARDONNAY

The junior member of the entourage. Appley, crisp. $9.

1993 PELLEGRINI VINTNER'S PRIDE CHARDONNAY

Among the oakier of Pellegrini's productions, the wine has hints of butterscotch, nuttiness, floral qualities and all-around richness. Fine acidity. It has a long, long finish. Balanced and fine. $20.

1993 PELLEGRINI CHARDONNAY

A light, good, round chardonnay, fruity and with crisp acidity at the outset. Some smoky qualities, too. Starting to show its age now. $13.

1996 PINDAR CHARDONNAY RESERVE

The barrel-fermented wine certainly is oaky, with a trace of butterscotch. But lighter than usual for a reserve. $15.

1996 PINDAR PEACOCK LABEL CHARDONNAY

Some touches of pear and tropical fruit in this crisp and easygoing white. A pleasant wine with veal, chicken. $11.

1995 PINDAR
CHARDONNAY RESERVE

A balanced, appley, barrel-fermented winner, refined and rather subtle, with very respectable varietal character. $15.

1994 PINDAR
CHARDONNAY RESERVE

Oak, vanilla and some upfront fruitiness are evident in this barrel-fermented wine. But short on ripeness and fullness. $15.

1995 PINDAR PEACOCK
LABEL CHARDONNAY

Balanced, fruity and lively, this wine has improved since its release. Drinking well now, as an accompaniment to light fare. $9.

1996 PINDAR SUNFLOWER
SPECIAL RESERVE
CHARDONNAY

The California style, but not overdone. The wine isn't as big as the '95 or the '94, which may disappoint Sunflower fans. But the fruitiness, tropical variety, is a plus. The wine has a vivid aroma. $17.

1995 PINDAR SUNFLOWER
SPECIAL RESERVE
CHARDONNAY

As oaky as the boldest, heavy-duty Californian, this is a wine for the palate enamored of the style. Buttery in the extreme, with some hints of pineapple. Have it with rich shellfish dishes. $17.

1994 PINDAR SUNFLOWER
CHARDONNAY

Full-bodied, mouth-filling and oakier than most Long Island chardonnays, this isn't a fruity, everyday glass of anonymity at all. The wine continues to show life. $16.

1995 PUGLIESE
CHARDONNAY RESERVE

A solid, quite dry, barrel-fermented wine that has a citrusy finish. $13.

1994 PUGLIESE
CHARDONNAY GOLD

An everyday chardonnay, pretty smooth and tank-fermented. $10.

1994 PUGLIESE
CHARDONNAY RESERVE

On the light side, easy-drinking, refreshing and good, with a fine finish. It has a trace of apple and a bit of spice, too. Ready for seafood. $13.

1995 SAGPOND WOLFFER
LA FERME MARTIN
CHARDONNAY

With this wine, "La Ferme" est finie. The last of this colorful label's bright, crisp and lemony chardonnays, the original white from Sagpond. It was named for Christian Wolffer's father. Future chardonnays are Wolffer, period. $13.

1994 SAGPOND WOLFFER
ESTATE CHARDONNAY

This white is a balanced and winning wine from the oldest section of the Sagaponack vineyard. It's lively, elegant, unfiltered and unfined wine, with plenty of spine, good acidity, toasty oak, and very rich suggestions of pear, lemon and honey. The wine at first seems Burgundian, then makes a turn toward California. Prepare your lobster dinner. $25.

1994 SAGPOND DOMAINE WOLFFER RESERVE CHARDONNAY
This unfined wine has a lovely gold color; ripe fruit; and more than a hint of apple, fig, melon. More Californian than Burgundian. Yeasty, velvety, with a hint of oak. $15.

1993 SAGPOND DOMAINE WOLFFER RESERVE CHARDONNAY
Medium-bodied, this is a leaner chardonnay, less intense than the one above, along the lines of a Chablis. Currently playing the back nine. $15.

Chenin Blanc

This is the grape of the Loire Valley, and of South Africa, where it used to be called steen. It has high acidity and is blended into wines still and sparkling, sweet and dry. But think mainly of Vouvray and Saumur. A fragrant choice, with one producer on Long Island. So far.

1997 PAUMANOK CHENIN BLANC
This winery has demonstrated with flair how well chenin blanc can work on Long Island. The dry delight from the '97 vintage has suggestions of citrus, mainly grapefruit. First-rate with sole or trout, oysters or scallops. $14.

1995 PAUMANOK CHENIN BLANC
A marvelous, summery wine, suggesting grapefruit. Balanced and enjoyable in its prime. But late for this vintage now. $10.

1994 PAUMANOK CHENIN BLANC
More acidic, lemony and tart than its successors. $8.

Gewürztraminer

Fragrant, floral and spicy, gewürztraminer is a very recognizable wine. Yet the grape yields wines with varied personalities. It can be vinified into a fruity or dry wine, or a viscous dessert wine. Gewürztraminer does best in Alsace, but also is grows in parts of California, the Pacific Northwest, and with some success on the East End.

1995 BEDELL GEWÜRZTRAMINER
Very good varietal character, with a rose-petal aroma. It doesn't overdo the spice and is richly satisfying, especially with Asian dishes. $10.

1994 BEDELL GEWÜRZTRAMINER
Some litchi does appear in the flavors of this wine, but overall, it seems more in neutral than high gear. $10.

1994 LENZ GEWÜRZTRAMINER
Dry, unusually crisp, subtly spicy, and quite good. Not overly intense, but fragrant, with a hint of grapefruit. $11.

1993 LENZ GEWÜRZTRAMINER
Lenz's lean gewürztraminers have been a benchmark for years; the winery's earlier efforts for a time seemed among the region's most distinctive whites. No surprise with this wine, handily among the best, with spice, overtones of pink grapefruit, style. $20.

1996 PALMER GEWÜRZTRAMINER
Very fruity, lighter and sweeter than the '95. But quite fragrant with spices. $15.

1995 PALMER GEWÜRZTRAMINER
Slightly citric and straightforward, with traces of litchi, this fragrant wine is well-balanced and refreshing. It has an attractive spiciness and works with seafood, Indian fare, Chinese food. $10.

Pinot Blanc

France, Germany and Italy are among the homes of pinot blanc. The grapes may be used in blending. But it's a brisk, lively varietal, acidic and not overpowering in flavor. The dry white wines never reach the complexity of chardonnay, but they're fresh and ideal in summer.

1995 HARGRAVE PINOT BLANC
Alsatian in style, with fine acidity and refreshing character. Very good all around. $10.

1996 PALMER LIEB VINEYARD PINOT BLANC
A versatile, minerally white wine. It's dry, crisp, refreshing, with a hint of melon. A quaffing wine to have with shellfish. The cooler season that led to the '96 vintage seems to have enlivened the wine. $11.

1996 PALMER ESTATE PINOT BLANC
Refreshing, crisp, uncomplicated and very good. $10.

1995 PALMER LIEB VINEYARD PINOT BLANC
Fresh, clean, with aspects of grapefruit. But softer than the snappy '96. $9.

1995 LENZ VINEYARD PINOT BLANC
This is dry, minerally, lean, expressive and very refreshing wine, with a hint of hazelnut. $11.

1994 LENZ VINEYARD PINOT BLANC
A very dry winner, breezy and clean, with the personality of peach, a touch of citrus, and nuances of tropical fruit. Perfect with shellfish. $13.

1993 LENZ VINEYARD PINOT BLANC
Memorable wine, dry and delightful. $13.

Riesling

The superior grape of Germany goes under many names and adapts to many styles. The sturdy vine has no problem with cooler climates. In Alsace, rieslings are made dry; in Germany, they're fruitier and more aromatic. As a late-harvest dessert wine, riesling reaches remarkable sweetness. In a time of chardonnay madness, riesling is a lovely counterpoint.

1995 BIDWELL DRY WHITE RIESLING
A change for this winery, vinifying its riesling dry. The wine is fine, in many ways more enjoyable than the semisweet variety. $13.

1995 BIDWELL WHITE RIESLING
The sweeter version, fruity and attractive, with suggestions of apricot, mango. $10.

1997 CHANNING PERRINE RIESLING
A dry, refreshing white with pleasing varietal character that develops slowly. Made with North Fork grapes. Not yet released.

1996 JAMESPORT RIESLING
Lighter than its predecessor, but also an appealing, soft and aromatic wine, with traces of orange and green apple. $12.

1995 JAMESPORT RIESLING
Lighthearted, but you may detect a lack of ripeness. Some peach and green-apple notes. A sipper. Chill it. $14.

1995 OSPREY'S DOMINION RIESLING
Peach and apricot in this creamy, delicate wine that's on the sweet side. Serve chilled. $10.

1997 PALMER WHITE RIESLING
This pleasurable wine immediately puts you in the mood for Memorial Day weekend. It comes at you with full fruit. The white riesling is more a sipper than a food wine, but you'll like it on a picnic. The wine includes a bit of viognier for an added dimension. $11.

1996 PALMER WHITE RIESLING
Not as ripe as the '97. $10.

1997 PAUMANOK RIESLING
This is a fruity, off-dry white, with an engaging and enticing floral aroma and a hint of quince. It's drier than the '96 riesling, and overall, better. Right with chicken, turkey, ham, or on its own. $14.

1996 PAUMANOK RIESLING
Floral, semi-dry, very good acidity, better than the '95. Try it with spicy food, or with sashimi and sushi. $12.

1995 PAUMANOK RIESLING
A semi-sweet wine, with aspects of tangelo and some tropical fruit. Meant to be drunk young, it's approaching senior status now. $11.

1995 PECONIC BAY WHITE RIESLING
Pretty sweet, with some

pineapple notes, but commendably clean and quite fruity. Time to prepare your picnic lunch. $11.

1996 PINDAR JOHANNISBERG RIESLING
The wine is rather sweet, with a trace of peach and melon. Right with chicken dishes or mild finfish. $9.

Sauvignon Blanc

High in acid and typically herbaceous, sauvignon blanc isn't a neutral wine. It shows off best in the Loire, with Sancerre and Pouilly-Fumé; in California, and New Zealand. The wines tend to be crisp. But this grape also can lead to remarkable dessert wines.

1996 BIDWELL SAUVIGNON BLANC
Crisp, citrusy, dry, and light-bodied, with accents of tropical fruit. The wine was aged on the lees for a while. Very good acidity, very good result. $17.

1995 BIDWELL SAUVIGNON BLANC
Excellent varietal character, a little grassy, citrusy, and herbal. Balanced and right. $18.

1997 CHANNING PERRINE SAUVIGNON BLANC
Crisp, refreshing and a candidate to accompany countless dishes of shellfish. Made from North Fork grapes. Tasted before bottling. Not yet released.

1996 HARGRAVE BLANC FUMÉ
Lemony, with a little pineapple, and more austere than the '95 sauvignon blanc. $11.

1995 HARGRAVE BLANC FUMÉ
A wonderful example of how sauvignon blanc can thrive on

Long Island. The color is a lovely pale yellow and the flavors are refreshing, from honeysuckle on. Fine acidity and no smokiness to distract you. Delicate and fruitier than the '94. $11.

1996 JAMESPORT SAUVIGNON BLANC
Light, green, certainly lemony, but it curiously lacks that vivid varietal character. An off-year option. $11.

1995 JAMESPORT SAUVIGNON BLANC
A grassy, respectable varietal, crisp, round and attractive. Herbal. Have it with seafood. $11.

1997 MACARI SAUVIGNON BLANC
A light, pleasant wine, with varietal character that makes you look forward to the next. $12.

1996 PALMER SAUVIGNON BLANC
The green grass and pungency of a Sancerre, if not the complexity, are in this refreshing wine. $9.

1995 PALMER SAUVIGNON BLANC

Crisp and herbal, it has the sort of varietal character that separates the lovers of this grape from the mere admirers. Zesty stuff. Try it with shellfish. $9.

1994 PALMER SAUVIGNON BLANC

This diverting wine was aromatic and attractive, fresh and fine when released. The acidity has since mellowed, and it's still drinking surprisingly well. $7.

White Blends and More

BEDELL CYGNET

Made with 80 per cent riesling and 20 per cent gewürztraminer, this casual sipper is refreshing and as sweet as it is dry. Picnics. $7.

BEDELL MAIN ROAD WHITE

The old truck on the label gives this wine an appropriately countrified image. Uncomplicated. $10.

DUCK WALK SOUTHAMPTON WHITE

A spirited, clean and refreshing white, made of chardonnay and a lot of pinot gris. Some grassiness. It should be popular throughout the summer. $8.

DUCK WALK WINDMILL WHITE

It's got aroma, from a union of chardonnay, riesling and pinot gris. But otherwise routine. Off-dry. $8.

GRISTINA AVALON

Mostly riesling, mainly sweet, with some muscat and upstate juice. Sold only at the winery. Chill it. Time for Chinese food. $8.

HARGRAVE DUNE BLANC

A genial blend of pinot blanc and chardonnay, in a light style. Satisfactory. $6.

JAMESPORT ISLAND BLANC

A casual wine, made primarily with sauvignon blanc. Off-dry and fruity. $10.

1995 PALMER SELECT RESERVE

An enticing wine made with 53 percent chardonnay, 21 percent sauvignon blanc, 15 percent gewürztraminer, and 11 percent pinot blanc. The gewürztraminer is the curve, providing a fruitier finish. A fine sipping wine. $12.

PAUMANOK FESTIVAL WHITE

The wine is a combo of sauvignon blanc, chenin blanc and riesling. A little sweet, a little spicy, with hints of pink grapefruit. Good with sweet and sour shrimp. $10.

PECONIC BAY CLASSIC WHITE

Semi-dry wine made with 95 per cent riesling, 5 per cent chardonnay. You'll detect pineapple and pear. Respectable with simple seafood dishes. $10.

1996 PECONIC BAY VIN DE L'ILE-BLANC

Fruity, semi-sweet, very casual: a wine-of-the-Island riesling. $10.

1996 PELLEGRINI EAST END SELECT COMMONAGE WHITE

Some name. Anyway, an off-dry sipper sold at the winery. Finger Lakes grapes make up almost half of it. Routine. $9.

1996 PINDAR VIOGNIER

Perfumed and lively with aspects of apricot and peach, light spices. Fine bouquet. Not yet released.

1995 PINDAR VIOGNIER

Floral and attractive, with a hint of peach. Unusual and worth sampling. $19.

PINDAR AUTUMN GOLD

A light, dry wine vaguely reminiscent of upstate blends. Minor. $8.

PINDAR WINTER WHITE

The mild combo of riesling, chardonnay and Cayuga, and a very modest sipper. $8. 🌰

CHAPTER 4

Enjoying the Classic Reds

Sometimes life is a cabernet

L ong Island is New York's haven for the classic red grape varieties, such as cabernet sauvignon and merlot. Red wines come in many shades, from the purplish tint of youth to the brick-red of maturity. The grapes themselves are reddish, and often closer to blue. Some look black.

Red wine gets its color when the juice of the grapes contacts the skins during fermentation. The skins also impart tannins, those compounds that give wine astringency and act as a preservative, lengthening its life.

In addition to cabernet sauvignon and merlot, red wine grapes include pinot noir, syrah, cabernet franc, gamay, nebbiolo, sangiovese, zinfandel and grenache.

Following are the main varieties of red wine made on Long Island, with reviews of the wines. Blends and varietals made in smaller quantities also are noted. Prices are subject to change.

Cabernet Franc

This grape long has been known as a blending companion for cabernet sauvignon, the greatest of red wine grapes. Cabernet franc is a popular, cool-weather planting in Bordeaux, the Loire Valley, southwest France and Italy. The summit of cabernet franc is attained by Chateau Cheval Blanc in Saint-Emilion. More of the variety is being planted on Long Island, where the climate and the soil suggest it has a good future. It may be the next big red.

1994 BIDWELL CABERNET FRANC
Cherry and raspberry come to mind with this wine, which has bright color and good flavor. $23.

1995 HARGRAVE CABERNET FRANC
Rich, with lots of dark fruit, spiciness, and an ideal expression of the varietal gone local. Part of the appeal of this wine is that it doesn't strive to be more than cabernet franc. Almost laid-back. $14.

1994 HARGRAVE CABERNET FRANC
Better than when released, this cabernet franc has opened up a bit. But it's still not too fruity. $13.

1993 HARGRAVE CABERNET FRANC
Some lively spiciness and raspberry notes define this aromatic, soft and accessible wine. Meant to be consumed young. Most has been. The medium-bodied wine goes well with seasoned lamb, pork, salmon. $14.

1995 JAMESPORT CABERNET FRANC
From the winery's Cutchogue vineyard, this is medium-bodied, minty, cedary, with a trace of cherry. Satisfying stuff. The wine is 20 percent cabernet sauvignon. And it could age a couple of years. $15.

1995 PALMER CABERNET FRANC
Full, ripe, soft, with traces of dried cherry and a singularly appealing aroma. Easily recommended. $16.

1994 PALMER CABERNET FRANC
Fruitier and earthier than the '93 cabernet franc, with blueberry notes. The wine is showing signs of fading now, but you still can detect the berry flavor. $14.

1993 PALMER CABERNET FRANC
A spirited red still drinking surprisingly well. Made with 14 percent merlot and 11 percent cabernet sauvignon, the wine is less herbaceous than usual. Light tannin. $14.

1995 PELLEGRINI CABERNET FRANC
Spiciness throughout this spirited and inviting medium-bodied wine. It has a full, tannic structure, and aspects of mint and raspberry. The varietal character is there, though not pronounced. A bigger version of the '94. $23.

**1994 PELLEGRINI
CABERNET FRANC**
Good varietal character,
soft and approachable, very
much upfront and satisfying.
$16.

**1994 PINDAR
CABERNET FRANC**
Some fruitiness is evident in
this respectable bottle, mainly
black cherry. It's peppery and
ripe. But the wine is getting
on. No aging required. Drink it
now. $17.

**1995 SCHNEIDER
CABERNET FRANC**
Better than the '94, with excellent varietal character, bright
color, and terrific appeal at the
table. Very smooth. Not yet
released.

**1994 SCHNEIDER
CABERNET FRANC**
A delightful debut for these
vintners. The wine is made
with Palmer Vineyard grapes
by Bedell Cellars. A harmonious union, with some spice
and personality. $19.

Cabernet Sauvignon

The grand grape of Bordeaux, cabernet sauvignon
yields those slowly-maturing complex wines of
legend, among them Chateaux Latour, Lafite-
Rothschild and Mouton-Rothschild. California's
noblest reds are cabernet sauvignon, too. The small,
blue-black, thick-skinned, low-yield grape ripens
late. So, a long growing season and warm weather
are essential. Well-drained soil helps, too. On Long
Island, cabernet sauvignon does well only in years
when hot weather persists. The '90s have been
uncommonly generous.

**1995 BEDELL
CABERNET SAUVIGNON**
Big, rich and terrific, with a
pretty long life ahead of it, this
cabernet ranks high in the
Bedell repertoire and bids fair
to be the winery's peak cabernet. Lots of black fruit character and spine. It's 10 percent
merlot. Drinking the cabernet
now would be snuffing out
potential. In time, it will compare very well with the pride of
California and with many
Bordeaux, and eclipse the '93.
Not yet released.

**1994 BEDELL
CABERNET SAUVIGNON**
The tannins are mellowing
and the fruit is ripe in this
well-orchestrated, full and
opulent production that leads
to a long, lovely finish. It
contains 2 percent merlot.
Cassis, mint, clove are evident. $19.

**1993 BEDELL
CABERNET SAUVIGNON**
Plenty of muscle in this vibrant
cabernet along with much
black fruit. Cassis and vanilla
are evident, along with a rare
sweetness from oak. The wine
includes 15 percent merlot. It
is maturing beautifully and
should be around for years in
your cellar. The finish is long.
$16.

1993 BIDWELL
CABERNET SAUVIGNON

The wine has gotten better with age, losing the tannic first impression that marked its release. The flavors are riper and the structure intact. Try it with a prime rib. Nothing light. $20.

1994 DUCK WALK
CABERNET SAUVIGNON

There are suggestions of black cherry in this no-nonsense red. It has smoothed out a bit in the last year. But this isn't a study in finesse. Still, a long finish. North Fork grapes. $19.

1993 DUCK WALK
CABERNET SAUVIGNON

A blunt and full-bodied red, with 75 percent cabernet sauvignon, 13 percent merlot and 12 percent cabernet franc. Pindar grapes are part of the mix. Subtle: no. It may age a while, however. $18.

1996 GRISTINA
CABERNET SAUVIGNON

Not on a par with the '95. An agreeable wine, but it doesn't have the tannic structure for a long life. Drink it now, while waiting for release of the 1993 Andy's Field Cabernet Sauvignon. $16.

1995 GRISTINA
CABERNET SAUVIGNON

You could contentedly be drinking this concentrated wine around the millennium and beyond. But the supply isn't likely to last that long. The supple, big red is fine now, too. This is 100 percent cabernet sauvignon, with excellent fruit and strength. But it's neither as lean nor as tannic as you'd expect, having properties associated more with merlots. Black currant and black cherry qualities. A first-class food wine to pair with beef and lamb. $16.

1993 GRISTINA
CABERNET SAUVIGNON

Depth and body, very concentrated, with nuances of currant and cedar. The wine is 88 percent cabernet sauvignon and 12 percent cabernet franc. First-rate food wine. $16.

1992 GRISTINA
CABERNET SAUVIGNON

Tannic at the start, this full-bodied cabernet has mellowed over the years, with suggestions of currant and coffee. Not great, but good. $14.

1993 HARGRAVE QED
CABERNET SAUVIGNON

As in "quod erat demonstrandrum." And, as the Latin phrase suggests, it has been shown: an assemblage extraordinaire. Tasted recently, not when released. It's a big, deep wine, with remarkable complexity and surely a local wine to bring in the new century. There's some briariness from cabernet franc, the blueberry of a ripe merlot, and the cassis, leathery contribution of cabernet sauvignon. All the elements came together with this one. Symphonic wine. $40.

HARGRAVE PETIT CHATEAU
CABERNET SAUVIGNON

An early-drinking, rather light, nonvintage wine that has the benefit of some oak with almost no tannin. A slight chill won't hurt it. $9.

1995 LAUREL LAKE
CABERNET SAUVIGNON

A bit closed and tannic at this point, but could soften in a year or two. Made at The Lenz Winery. $24.

1995 LENZ
CABERNET SAUVIGNON

A big, extracted wine with plenty of aging potential, fine-tuned with merlot. The fruit is exceptional. It should be among the vintage's top cabernets. It at first seems like Napa Valley east. Not yet released.

1994 LENZ
CABERNET SAUVIGNON

Cassis, black currants, vanilla, oak play off each other in this excellent, concentrated garnet-shaded cabernet. That's a suggestion of raspberry in the aroma. Almost one-quarter cabernet franc. $25.

1993 LENZ
CABERNET SAUVIGNON

An assertively earthy cabernet that carries with it a surprising touch of sweetness. There's diverting complexity here: a wine that unfolds slowly and is very rewarding in the process. From such a French-styled winery, surprisingly Californian. Excellent. $20.

1996 LOUGHLIN
CABERNET SAUVIGNON

The wine has good color. But it's rather tight and sharp, as if short on ripeness. It needs to smooth out. A year or two in the bottle may help. $17.

1995 OSPREY'S DOMINION
RESERVE CABERNET
SAUVIGNON

Big and bold, this cabernet spent 18 months in oak barrels and has firm structure, fine fruit, potential for a long stay. Keep it for a while and you'll be rewarded. It includes 15 percent merlot. $25.

1995 OSPREY'S DOMINION
CABERNET SAUVIGNON

A medium-bodied and slightly tannic wine that will require some patience, though not as much as the reserve. Spicy and dense, the wine has overtones of licorice, black pepper, cherry. $15.

1993 OSPREY'S DOMINION
CABERNET SAUVIGNON

Oakier and fruitier than the '95, and not as intense. It has some cherry notes. $15.

1995 PALMER
CABERNET SAUVIGNON

This is a very smooth, round red, right for drinking now though it should mature well, too. The wine is 75 percent cabernet sauvignon, 20 percent merlot, and 5 percent cabernet franc. It has good, berry fruit and a big tannic structure. $15.

1994 PALMER
CABERNET SAUVIGNON

Medium-bodied with a definite cherry overlay. The tannins are smooth and the wine drinkable for some time. It's 83 percent cabernet sauvignon, 15 percent merlot, and 2 percent cabernet franc. $13.

1993 PALMER
CABERNET SAUVIGNON

A medium-bodied wine that has developed very well, with a fine overlay of cherry. It has 15 percent merlot and 2 percent cabernet franc. Balanced and smooth, with some time ahead of it. $13.

1995 PAUMANOK TUTHILLS LANE LIMITED EDITION CABERNET SAUVIGNON

This stunner is a Bordeaux vacationing on the East End. It should have a long stay in cellars, though there probably aren't many bottles left to buy. The tannins are firm and the flavors concentrated. The excellent fruit is only the start. This cabernet has great depth and style, and will age gracefully. Elegance and power: a Sugar Ray of a wine. $39.

1995 PAUMANOK GRAND VINTAGE CABERNET SAUVIGNON

Excellent cabernet sauvignon, potent and lush, full of fruit and minty fragrance. The tannins are there, but only to complement. The wine has wonderfully rich mouth-feel. Age-worthy for sure. It has many qualities of the Limited Edition wine, if not the knockout. $19.

1994 PAUMANOK CABERNET SAUVIGNON

Lighter, with suggestions of black currant, some cherry. For drinking now. $13.

1993 PAUMANOK GRAND VINTAGE CABERNET SAUVIGNON

The tannins have softened in this commendable, red-purple cabernet, which is as recommended now as it is difficult to locate. It has 10 percent cabernet franc. Enjoy the blackberry flavors and the suggestions of plum. Toasty oak, ripe fruit. A long finish. $22.

1995 PECONIC BAY CABERNET SAUVIGNON

A full-bodied, solid, aromatic ruby-hued cabernet, with fine fruit and firm tannins. Very satisfying, and it should last several years. $22.

1994 PECONIC BAY CABERNET SAUVIGNON

A blunt red that has matured nicely since release, with tannins smoothed somewhat. Full and satisfying, with suggestions of blackberry. Have it now with hearty stews, beef and lamb, red-sauced meals. $30.

1995 PELLEGRINI CABERNET SAUVIGNON

Very big, deep, ripe red, with excellent structure, firm tannins, cassis and dark fruit character. Lots of time ahead. Tasted early, the wine does need more time to evolve. But it has the potential to be exceptional. The wine includes 11 percent cabernet franc and 4 percent merlot. Wonderful wine. Not yet released.

1994 PELLEGRINI CABERNET SAUVIGNON

A balanced, unfiltered wine that's softened by 11 percent cabernet franc and 4 percent merlot. It's a well-structured, full-bodied number, slightly tannic, with ample fruit suggesting plum, and some spiciness. Ripe and right with roast beef and lamb. $15.

1993 PELLEGRINI CABERNET SAUVIGNON

Excellent wine, dark and intense, with generous fruit. Traces of cassis and mint. There's more than enough oak and tannin, too. The wine still has a year or more before it hits its peak. Worth seeking. $15.

1994 PINDAR CABERNET SAUVIGNON

A straightforward red, rough around the edges, and a little astringent. $19.

1993 PINDAR RESERVE CABERNET SAUVIGNON

The concentrated, heavy-duty, dry wine has gotten better since its release, with softer tannins. The fruit shows through these days, with cherry the leader. $17.

1995 PUGLIESE CABERNET SAUVIGNON

Some cabernet franc is blended into this no-nonsense red. Save it for a hearty meal. $14.

1994 PUGLIESE CABERNET SAUVIGNON RESERVE

For your sturdiest fare, this is a gutsy red. It may smooth slightly over time. $14.

1993 PUGLIESE CABERNET SAUVIGNON

It's 100 percent cabernet sauvignon and lets you know it point blank. Blunt red wine, medium-bodied and made for steaks, chops, red-sauce dishes. $14.

1995 TERNHAVEN CABERNET SAUVIGNON

Improves significantly on the '94, with deeper flavors and more structure. But not too smooth. Made at Pellegrini Vineyards. $16.

1994 TERNHAVEN CABERNET SAUVIGNON

Short on good fruit and more than a little acidic, this is a rough early effort from a new winery. Made at Pellegrini Vineyards. $16.

Merlot

The grape that has reined in white-wine drinkers and attracted many others to reds, merlot is much softer and less tannic and demanding than cabernet sauvignon. It has been the primary blending grape for cabernet sauvignon in Bordeaux and the most planted. In the cooler regions of Bordeaux, Pomerol and Saint-Emilion, the thin-skinned merlot is the main red grape. Chateau Petrus is made with merlot. This is a dependable varietal in Italy, California, Washington and definitely on Long Island. It ripens earlier than cabernet sauvignon and is the East End's most reliable red.

1995 BEDELL MERLOT RESERVE

A bright star of the vintage, full-bodied and a trifle tannic now. But concentrated and rich, with the vividness of black fruit and ample oak. Excellent varietal character. The color is marvelous, with a hint of purple in the dark ruby shade. The wine should last a while. $28.

1995 BEDELL MERLOT
The first notable red from Bedell's '95 vintage is a supple, ripe and fruity wine. It carries a suggestion of plum and cherry. Drinkable now, the wine also should improve over the next year or two. The merlot is an ideal food wine. Try it with grilled tuna. $18.

1994 BEDELL MERLOT RESERVE
The wine, marvelous when released, continues to get better, with full fruit and the seductive appeal of a work in progress. Not a blockbuster like the predecessor and successor, but an elegant, middleweight wine that should last a long time. Enjoy the cherry flavors. $28.

1994 BEDELL MERLOT
An intensely fragrant wine, but not exactly upfront in its fruitiness. Elegant and lean, Bordeaux in style. And one that continues to make for very good drinking. Have it with red meat. $16.

1993 BEDELL MERLOT RESERVE
A mouthful. Here's an extraordinary red to reckon with, big and beautiful, with loads of fruit and enough tannin to give it a substantial life. You'll like it now. But the supple and elegant wine continues to improve. Expect it to do so for several years. $28.

1993 BEDELL MERLOT
The wine is better now than when released a few years ago. And it could last another two or three. The berry-like flavor continues and the finish is long. Much of this wine was consumed early. You'll have to look around. $16.

1993 BIDWELL MERLOT
Plummy, ruby-shaded, somewhat smoky, this unfiltered wine has a long finish and ripely represents the fruit. It's 20 percent cabernet sauvignon and 5 percent cabernet franc. Have a barbecue. $20.

1995 CHANNING DAUGHTERS SCULPTURE GARDEN MERLOT
The first red from this winery is very closed now. It needs some time. Made for Channing Daughters by The Lenz Winery. $17.

1996 COREY CREEK MERLOT
Satisfying, medium-bodied, lighter and more modest than the previous vintages. It has good color, suggestions of black cherry, and very respectable varietal character, drinking well now. $18.

1995 COREY CREEK MERLOT
A stylish, recommended red, with loads of fruit and hints of oak. Immediately more accessible than the '94. It's 88 percent merlot, 6 percent cabernet franc and 6 percent cabernet sauvignon. Very smooth, and pairing nicely with roast veal and roast duck. Made at Pellegrini Vineyards. $18.

1994 COREY CREEK MERLOT
An attractive, enticing, round wine, with an undercurrent of red berries and herbs. It has

matured nicely, with softening tannins, and continues to drink with flair. The wine is 81 percent merlot, 14 percent cabernet franc, 5 percent cabernet sauvignon. Made at Pellegrini Vineyards. $17.

1993 COREY CREEK MERLOT
You'll mistake it for a full-blown California merlot, spurred by ripe fruit and the right amount of oak. The polished wine is 80 percent merlot, 15 percent cabernet franc, and 5 percent cabernet sauvignon. Drinking just fine. Lovely if you can spot it somewhere. Made at Pellegrini Vineyards. $16.

1995 DUCK WALK RESERVE MERLOT
Tight right now, with the fruit hidden. But the aroma is enticing and the oakiness is held in check. The wine has a nice, plummy cast and offers potential. Give it some time, or sausages and peppers. $15.

1994 DUCK WALK RESERVE MERLOT
An unfiltered, medium-bodied wine, but in a very soft style, with the flavor of black fruit. Good drinking now, especially if your dinner is beef, duck or red-sauced. $19.

1994 DUCK WALK MERLOT
Rounder, fruitier, softer than the '94 reserve. The styles are very different. Wine for hamburger, medium-rare. $17.

1995 GRISTINA MERLOT
On a par with the fine '93 merlot, from the terrific vintage. It has body, backbone, very good fruit, and should last a

while. You'll like it now, too. $15.

1994 GRISTINA ANDY'S FIELD MERLOT
Excellent, high concentration of fruit in this wine, with plenty of berry, cherry, spice, and tannins that are giving it a good, long life as well as complexity. You can drink this one for years to come. $27.

1994 GRISTINA MERLOT
Very good, soft and ripe, with suggestions of sweet cherries. The supple wine has herbal nuances, too. Food wine. $15.

1993 GRISTINA ANDY'S FIELD MERLOT
A potent, deeply-colored, concentrated and tannic single-vineyard merlot that has softened and become more accessible. One of the outstanding reds of the year. The black fruit is here, as are hints of vanilla. All is in harmony, aging well. $27.

1993 GRISTINA MERLOT
Lots of cherry, blackberry, and currant in this full-bodied, concentrated wine that continues show its attractiveness. Maybe, a sirloin. $15.

1995 HARGRAVE LATTICE LABEL MERLOT
Merlot with complexity, harmony and excellent varietal character. Violet and vivid. This is a medium-bodied number. It contains some cabernet sauvignon and could thrive for a decade. $18.

1994 HARGRAVE MERLOT
Soft, full of fruit, very accessible, and one destined immediately for the table instead of

the cellar. Roast that duck.
$16.

1993 HARGRAVE LATTICE LABEL MERLOT

Fine drinking now for this serious, first-class wine that ranks high in Hargrave history and wears the lattice label like a crown. A fruity and very satisfying red that has the textbook union of plums and blackberries. $28.

1995 JAMESPORT CHURCH FIELD MERLOT

The equivalent of a reserve wine, this very good merlot comes from Jamesport's older vines. Fruity, plummy, but with some spine. $18.

1995 JAMESPORT ESTATE MERLOT

Could be smoother, but a good, pretty fruity, workmanlike merlot for current drinking. $16.

1994 JAMESPORT ESTATE MERLOT

Soft, accessible, satisfactory, uncomplicated. The ruby-hued wine has a hint of raspberry and a lush bouquet. Drinking well now. $16.

1993 JAMESPORT MERLOT RESERVE

The leading candidate for best red produced at Jamesport, this merlot has fine varietal character, firmness, ripeness of fruit. You'll enjoy it now, but it could last longer. $20.

1995 LENZ ESTATE BOTTLED MERLOT

Deep and delicious, a masterful marriage of berry fruit and just the right amount of oak. You'll be tempted to drink it all

now, but some patience will be generously rewarded. Very impressive. Not yet released.

1994 LENZ ESTATE BOTTLED MERLOT

Sumptuous, opulent, ripe with black fruit, and headed for a good, long life. But the upfront pleasures of this wine are such that most of it will be consumed very soon. Be patient. You want to linger with the wine when its fully mature. $30.

1993 LENZ ESTATE BOTTLED MERLOT

A superb wine. Reductive flavors are the undercurrent of this merlot, which also has the requisite plumminess and wonderful fruit. The tannins are soft and the berries are evident. Still drinking nicely, as it should be, the wine also will last a while. $25.

1996 MACARI MERLOT

Respectable beginning, but young and rather closed at this point. $16.

1995 OSPREY'S DOMINION MERLOT

Fruity and fairly light, with good varietal character, traces of plum. Not for storage. It's drinking well now. $15.

1993 OSPREY'S DOMINION MERLOT

The wine has engaging spiciness, oakiness, grapeyness and is a high-octane production that stands out with food instead of alone. It has mellowed. Made at Palmer Vineyards. $14.

PALMER MERLOT

This nonvintage wine resulted

from the slow-ripening '96 harvest, and is a little rough. Red-meat wine. It has been supplemented by lots from '95 and '97. $14.

1995 PALMER RESERVE MERLOT

An accessible, jammy, ripe, wine that's another advertisement for the outstanding vintage. Lots of plum, prune and cherry character are in it, and there's also a pleasant undercurrent of spiciness, and heavy oak. A long finish. Drinking it now wouldn't be infanticide, give it another year or two to enjoy the expected softening of the wine. $29.

1995 PALMER MERLOT

Lighter than the reserve, the garnet wine is fairly fruity despite the occasional tannic interruptions. It's 100 percent merlot and a supple, accessible red, with peppery notes along with the black fruit, and a floral aroma. Your reliable food wine. $16.

1994 PALMER MERLOT

A neat balance of sweet fruit and oak, round and attractive. Very good, with hints of raspberry. Not as intense as the '93 and the '95. It's 100 percent merlot. $15.

1995 PAUMANOK GRAND VINTAGE MERLOT

A slow starter, but evolving into a marvelous wine, heady with varietal character. A velvety finish. Opening up now, with much potential for the long haul. $22.

1993 PAUMANOK GRAND VINTAGE MERLOT

Neatly balanced wine, with

lots of blackberry and spice. It has considerable depth and continues to drink well. $19.

1995 PECONIC BAY EPIC ACRE MERLOT

This is the best wine produced at Peconic Bay, red or white. It's full-bodied with excellent fruit and plenty of spine, and a stirring shade of ruby en route to black. Peconic Bay's most intense merlot by far. The acre in question is visible from the tasting room and is a carefully tended spot. It shows. The 100 percent merlot has the benefits of oak. Very ripe with black fruit. $25.

1995 PECONIC BAY MERLOT

The tannins come up on you here. But the medium-bodied wine does have good fruit and concentrated flavors. $20.

1994 PECONIC BAY WESLEY HALL MERLOT

Sturdy, lively, ripe, with softening tannins, this is a respectable merlot for drinking now. Good accompaniment for dishes from roast chicken to pizza. $20.

1993 PECONIC BAY MERLOT

A fruity, amply berried wine that's medium-bodied, still a little tannic, and about as mature as it's going to get. Get the pepperoni on half the pizza. $15.

1995 PELLEGRINI MERLOT

Wonderful color, in the dark ruby range, and loaded with cherries, mint, and black fruit. The wine has great structure. The tannins are assertive, but should soften in time. It delivers in every way. $17.

1994 PELLEGRINI MERLOT

Very easy drinking with this full, fruity and fragrant merlot. Soft, plummy, with some blueberry character. A textbook example of the varietal's appeal, it will be gone before you know it. If you've got a bottle, keep it a year. One of their best. $17.

1993 PELLEGRINI MERLOT

A big, tannic merlot with unfolding elegance. It has grand berry glavors and generous ripeness. Drinking well, but you should hold onto the wine for a few years to savor it. $17.

1994 PINDAR RESERVE MERLOT

Balanced, with black cherry, the '94 is an accessible bottle at first. But it's a little astringent. $19.

1993 PINDAR RESERVE MERLOT

Much better than when released, the oaky, full-bodied wine has softened considerably. Plums are abundant. A good, smooth merlot. $15.

1995 PUGLIESE MERLOT

A satisfying, workmanlike merlot, with good fruit and no claims to complexity. $14.

1994 PUGLIESE MERLOT RESERVE

Good and flavorful, right with food. Not an intense wine, but it has a personality. $14.

1993 PUGLIESE MERLOT RESERVE

More fruity than tannic, this 100 percent merlot is defined by a subtle sweetness. Immediately approachable and enjoyable, whether you're eating steak, meatloaf or a good pizza. $14.

1995 SAGPOND WOLFFER ESTATE MERLOT

A marvelous merlot, with depth and finesse, among the leading reds from this South Fork winery. It's a sumptuous, opulent red, with excellent varietal character and the structure for a pretty long life. $29.

1995 SAGPOND WOLFFER MERLOT

This ripe, balanced, unfiltered and unfined wine is 85 percent merlot, 6 percent cabernet franc and, in an unusual addition, 3 percent pinot noir. It's not your basic, plummy LI merlot. Deep color, berries, anise, oakiness in the finish. $19.

1994 SAGPOND MERLOT

The wine was in oak for 16 months, and it had an early hardness. But it has mellowed and improved since its release. Drinking fairly well now. $14.

1994 SCHNEIDER MERLOT

Tasty, ripe, attractive, seamless wine from the new vintners, with fine fruit and considerable style. Made at Bedell Cellars from Macari Vineyards' grapes. $19.

1995 TERNHAVEN MERLOT

Much better than the vineyard's ho-hum '94 merlot, this wine has upfront fruit, mainly berries. Not great, but good. $18.

Pinot Noir

The temperamental, finicky, seductive grape of Burgundy also makes the base wine for Champagne. Not as tannic as cabernet sauvignon, it produces wines of many styles, with the heights reached in the wines of the Romanée-Conti estate. Pinot gris and pinot blanc are among its mutations. The grape buds early, needs good drainage, and doesn't yield a lot. You need luck as well as talent. Vines are planted in the Pacific Northwest and in some parts of Long Island, where as Alex Hargrave once said, "We're working on the luck."

1995 HARGRAVE PINOT NOIR 'LE NOIRIEN'
A superb, silky, elegant red from a grape that can be difficult. The name is from the old title for pinot noir in Burgundy. The wine has wonderful hints of black cherry and spice. Supple and distinctive. $35.

1994 HARGRAVE FLEURETTE
Pinot noir lite, more along the lines of a Beaujolais and quite pleasant. $9.

1993 HARGRAVE PINOT NOIR 'LE NOIRIEN'
Rich, opulent, soft, terrific pinot noir, still fabulous drinking. Burgundian all the way and handily among the finest wines made by Hargrave, or any other local winery. Check the archives. $35.

1994 GRISTINA PINOT NOIR
Very good and inviting pinot noir, with an undertone of cola and earthiness more than any upfront fruit. There's a hint of violet as a lagniappe. $25

1993 GRISTINA PINOT NOIR
An earthy, woodsy wine with a suggestion of mushrooms, cherries, blackberries, cola. The aromas are subtle and increasingly floral. When last tasted, the fruitiness was emerging nicely. $25.

1995 LENZ PINOT NOIR
The wine sometimes suggests those of the Pacific Northwest almost as much as Burgundy. It's very good, with fullness in the mouth-feel and considerable depth. Softer and not as reductive as the '93. But the wine does grab you. $15.

1993 LENZ PINOT NOIR
Mushrooms abound in this forest of a wine, which hints of dried fruits and the good earth. It's marvelous stuff, a journey in a bottle to which you'll want to return often, enjoying the new twists and turns. $25.

1996 OSPREY'S DOMINION PINOT NOIR
Medium-bodied and light on the tannin, this is a satisfying and forward pinot noir. There are suggestions of currant in it. If you like it, you like it a lot. $16.

1995 SAGPOND WOLFFER PINOT NOIR
An elegant, remarkable, full-bodied red, made from grapes grown by Atlantic Vineyards in Manorville. The color is deep

and so's the flavor, mainly dried cherry and plum. It's Wolffer's last pinot noir for a while. And it's just grand, whetting curiosity for what's ahead. $35.

Red Blends and More

1994 BEDELL CUPOLA
The newest of Bedell's adventures, the winery's first big red blend, Cupola is a marriage of cabernet sauvignon, cabernet franc and merlot, and a wine designed to last. $25.

BEDELL MAIN ROAD RED
Wine to uncork for the grill, with a label that portrays a vintage pick-up truck. It's not a bumpy ride. The blend includes merlot and cabernet sauvignon. Make it a cheese-burger. $10.

DUCK WALK GATSBY RED
Love that name and the label, too. The wine, a lesser Bordeaux-style blend, is a dry counterpart to the winery's Sweet Scarlett. Not the smoothest bottle. Right with a slice of Sicilian pizza on Daisy's dock. $9.

1995 DUCK WALK PINOT MEUNIER
You have to go far to find this varietal anywhere else; California, Australia, and some parts of Germany. It's one of the grapes used to make Champagne. But solo, pinot meunier is rare. The wine has traces of plum. Distinctively fruity taste. $13.

DUCK WALK WINDMILL RED
Do you want anchovies on that pizza? They made this wine with cabernet franc, cabernet sauvignon and pinot noir. Not much harmony. A country red that doesn't mind a little chill. $9.

JAMESPORT ISLAND ROUGE
A gamay and pinot noir blend that at its best suggests a standard Beaujolais. $10.

1994 JAMESPORT MELANGE DE TROIS
Mostly cabernet franc, with 20 percent divided equally between cabernet sauvignon and merlot. It's a tasty, mouth-filling blend: sample with robust fare. $16.

1993 JAMESPORT MELANGE DE TROIS
The wine doesn't quite har-monize, and seems tired save for a touch of spiciness. $16.

1992 JAMESPORT MELANGE DE TROIS
A Bordeaux-style red with a fairly short life. Time has run out. $15.

1993 PALMER SELECT RESERVE
The union's leader is cabernet sauvignon, at 56 percent, with about a third merlot and some cabernet franc. They harmo-nize well, buttressed by oak. The tannins have softened, but they're still assertive. Savor the long finish. Complex, still growing. $20.

1991 PALMER SELECT RESERVE
The heady alliance this time

is 70 percent cabernet sauvignon, 24 percent merlot and 6 percent cabernet franc. Drinking very well now. The tannin isn't so pronounced and the wine has an added richness. $20.

1995 PAUMANOK ASSEMBLAGE

The blend of this beauty is 55 percent cabernet sauvignon, 35 percent merlot, and 10 percent cabernet franc. It puts the "merit" in meritage. A fine balance of fruit and tannin that should appeal to the oak-oriented palate. $24.

1993 PAUMANOK ASSEMBLAGE

An excellent, harmonious blend, loaded with flavors of blackberry and black cherry. Some mintiness, too. The fruit and the tannin don't do battle. It's 45 percent cabernet sauvignon, 45 percent merlot, 10 percent cabernet franc. $22.

PECONIC BAY CLASSIC RED

Cabernet franc is the core of this fruity, in-your-face red that asks little. Some merlot in the blend, too. For immediate consumption. Who gets the Margherita? $11.

1995 PELLEGRINI VINTNER'S PRIDE ENCORE

Peak Pellegrini, and a bigger version of the '93. This opulent wine is maturing into an integrated, and long-lived Bordelaise blend, with backbone and character. Great color and fruit, full flavor, elegant structure. Tasted early. It has years of maturity ahead. Not yet released.

1994 PELLEGRINI VINTNER'S PRIDE ENCORE

Full-bodied, concentrated, supple, balanced and very Bordelaise, the wine is a bit earthy and should mature nicely for the next five years. The wine spent two years in French oak. The '94 is 53 percent cabernet sauvignon, 32 percent merlot, and 15 percent cabernet franc. Terrific with red meat. $24.

1993 PELLEGRINI VINTNER'S PRIDE ENCORE

Black cherry is the lingering fruit in this big, extremely good wine, which has a light oaky overlay. The tannins that marked its arrival have mellowed. It could last longer for sure, but this encore is ready to perform now. Another wine to have with red meat. $20.

1992 PELLEGRINI VINTNER'S PRIDE ENCORE

The '92 version is 62 percent cabernet sauvignon, 33 percent merlot, and 5 percent cabernet franc. And 100 percent enjoyable. Aspects of cassis. The red-meat wine is close to peak form now. Tasty with cheeses, too. $20.

1996 PELLEGRINI EAST END SELECT RED

Your basic, easydrinking table wine, with some pepperiness. Time for burgers, ribs, barbecued chicken. $10.

1996 PINDAR GAMAY BEAUJOLAIS

The fruity, upfront wine is a versatile player, with touches of raspberry. Have it chilled with chicken, hamburgers, three-alarm chili. The label is fun. So's the wine. $9.

1995 PINDAR MYTHOLOGY

Complex and inviting, this is peak Pindar. The Bordeaux blend, led by cabernet franc, is rich with taste from berries to cherries. There's a touch of oakiness and some spice, too. The finish is long, as should be the life of the wine. You could drink it now. But be patient for a couple of years. It will be worth the wait. Meantime, search for earlier vintages. You'll be very satisfied. $37.

1994 PINDAR MYTHOLOGY

The Bordeaux blend of this Mythology includes 26 percent petit verdot, which usually contributes to deep and full wines. The wine from this vintage certainly is both. Toastiness from the oak and a whiff of cherry are evident. The rest of the blend is 24 percent malbec, 20 percent cabernet sauvignon, 15 percent merlot and 15 percent cabernet franc. Lush and ripe. $25.

PINDAR SWEET SCARLETT

Semi-sweet, made with cabernet franc and some pinot noir. Tannins banished. The label looks like a view of the winery from Tara. Serve cold, with barbecued stuff. $9.

1997 PINDAR SYRAH

Syrah, the grape of the Rhône Valley and, as shiraz, of Australia, gets localized. The wine was tasted early. It has considerable body, and a smoky, cedary quality. Not yet released.

PUGLIESE RED TABLE WINE

Admire the bluntness of the name. It's more friendly than "meritage" and so's the wine, made with merlot and cabernet sauvignon. Picnics, barbecues. $8.

1996 PUGLIESE ZINFANDEL

You have to love Pugliese just for trying this varietal on Long Island; it thrives in California but doesn't really have the ideal climate here. The zinfandel is a grab-you, medium-bodied wine, with traces of spiciness. $15.

1995 TERNHAVEN CLARET D'ALVAH

The witty name underscores the owners' affection for the U.K. and the location of the vineyard on Alvah's Lane. Better than the '94. But still not so smooth. $18.

1994 TERNHAVEN CLARET D'ALVAH

Rough and acidic. $18.

CHAPTER 5

Sweet, Sparkling & More

A wine for every glass

This chapter covers a lot of vines and many different wines. We'll start with rosé and blush wines, those pretty-in-pink productions that are so right, chilled on a summer day.

Rosé wines are made from red grapes, but the contact between juice and skin is minimal. So they're the sort of red wines you can serve kind of like white wines. Rosés may be semi-sweet or, in their best form, dry.

Blush wine is an American term. These sweetish wines also are generally made from red grapes and there's only slight contact between the grape juice and the skins.

After rosés and blushes, we'll move on to sparkling wines, Long Island's bubbly variations on Champagne. Then the reviews turn to dessert wines, among which Long Island has many winners; local riffs on Port; and some fruity curiosities. The prices listed may change.

Rosé and Blush

BIDWELL COUNTRY GARDENS BLUSH
A sweetish, seasonal choice that's an alternative to white zinfandels. $7.

1997 COREY CREEK ROSÉ
Excellent dry rosé, different in style and better overall than the commendable '96. One of the top rosés made on the East End. $11.

1996 COREY CREEK ROSÉ
Fruity, full, and delightful, hosting suggestions of apple and berries. Spirited color, a pleasing wine. $10.

DUCK WALK WINDMILL BLUSH
The color is festive in this distant cousin of white zinfandel. A minor wine. $8.

1997 GRISTINA ROSÉ OF CABERNET SAUVIGNON
Plenty of fruit and fragrance in this dry, consistently appealing rosé. Pretty color, too. Made for a mid-summer day, it nevertheless has the flavor of the big grape. $9.

1996 GRISTINA ROSÉ OF CABERNET SAUVIGNON
Lively when released, the wine is about at its end. But it has more life than most local rosés even now. $9.

HARGRAVE DUNE BLUSH
Among the few blush wines that won't make you turn red with embarrassment. Dune Blush is a blend of pinot blanc and pinot noir. It's on the dry side, and a light sipper for a summer day. After all, there's a beach scene on the label. $6.

JAMESPORT ISLAND ROSÉ
Semi-sweet, from pinot noir and gamay. Serve ice cold. $10.

LAUREL LAKE LAKE ROSÉ
Satisfactory off-dry rosé, with some good fruit. Chill away. $10.

LAUREL LAKE WIND SONG
Perfumed name but little else. A minor project, with a taste of the Finger Lakes. You can serve it cold. $8.

1996 LENZ BLANC DE NOIR
A distinctive blush that's 100 per cent pinot noir. Better than most. For summertime. $8.

LOUGHLIN SOUTH BAY BREEZE BLUSH
Lighthearted, semi-sweet sipper. Chill it for a beach day. The label grabs you. $9.

1997 MACARI ROSÉ D'UNE NUIT
A dry, satisfying rosé, neatly styled. Very good first effort. $11.

OSPREY'S DOMINION TWILIGHT BLUSH
Made mainly with riesling, plus pinot noir and a little chardonnay. A standard-issue, summery sipper, quite sweet. $8.

PALMER SUNRISE SUNSET
Swiftly go the bottles, available in the tasting room only. A blushing mix, no more. $9.

1997 PAUMANOK VIN ROSÉ
This was Paumanok's first

contribution from the '97 vintage. The fruity wine is made with cabernet sauvignon, in a style that goes well with spicy dishes. $13.

PECONIC BAY BLUSH
More sweet than dry, made with riesling. Tutti frutti for hot weather. $9.

PINDAR SPRING SPLENDOR
Yes, that is cranberry you're tasting. Serve cold. $8.

PINDAR SUMMER BLUSH
The Suffolk Red grape makes its splash in this strawberry-shaded sipper. Spicy food alert. $9.

PUGLIESE BLUSH TABLE WINE
Niagara, with some merlot. Not the winery's best. $8.

1996 SAGPOND WOLFFER ROSÉ
Here's a bone-dry rosé, with a trace of apple and some citrus character, too. It's 42 percent chardonnay, 36 percent cabernet franc, 18 percent merlot. The shade is light salmon. The fruit is subtle. $10.

1995 SAGPOND WOLFFER ROSÉ
Very dry, very rosy, and balanced. But it's time for the curtain to fall. $9.

Sparkling Wine

JAMESPORT GRAND CUVÉE
A dry sparkler with plenty of bubbles. Good enough, but not really grand. It's made mainly with chardonnay, plus a fifth of pinot noir and gamay, which sweetens things too much. $19.

1993 LENZ CUVÉE
This wine was tasted before its release. The elegantly finished production is 70 per cent pinot noir and 30 per cent chardonnay. The salmon-colored '93 Cuvée is toasty, creamy and exceptional in a full, dry and rich blanc de noir style. Look for it. $20.

1991 LENZ CUVÉE
A delightul, delicate and yeasty sparkling wine that compares favorably with California's best bruts but has a lot in common with many true Champagnes. It's gold, light-bodied, toasty, and exceedingly dry. The Cuvée is a composition of chardonnay and pinot noir, and displays the charms of each. $20.

1992 PALMER BRUT
The combination is 60 percent pinot noir, 35 percent chardonnay and 5 percent pinot blanc — that two-thirds red, one-third white assemblage in certain Champagnes. The pinot noir from a cool year provides crispness. An attractive, dry sparkler that suggests Palmer will do well with the style for years. $20.

1994 PINDAR CUVÉE RARE
A very good sparkler, the most stylish from this producer. It has a pale straw color, yeastiness, and effervescence to spare. The dry, dry wine is 100 percent pinot

meunier, which alone makes it indeed rare. $28.

1995 PUGLIESE SPARKLING MERLOT
Here's a taste of nostalgia, sure to be enjoyed by those who adore fizzy reds and the flavors of the `50s table. It's exuberantly grapey, and bubbly in the extreme; opening the bottle can be a volcanic experience. The sweetish wine is billed as Pugliese's "red Champagne." It won't remind you of Dom Perignon Rosé, but it's fun. $18.

1995 PUGLIESE BLANC DE NOIR NATURE
Very dry, and good. The salmon-shaded bubbly is made entirely with pinot noir. $18.

1993 PUGLIESE BLANC DE BLANC
A good sparkler, in the brut mode, made with chardon-nay. The wine is on the light side, uncomplicated and straightforward in its Gallic approach and flavors. Enjoyable and very bubbly. $16.

1994 SAGPOND WOLFFER CUVEE
A full, heavier style of sparkling wine, quite rich and decidedly different from the '93. Creamier and more intense, not quite as yeasty. Depends on your preference in style. But fine. $34.

1993 SAGPOND WOLFFER CUVEE
With this brut, let's start at the finish: pear, apple, some citrus, and later, biscuit. Sagpond's first sparkler is creamy and has a trace of nuttiness in the flavor. It's 90 percent chardonnay and 10 percent pinot noir. For drinking now. Not an epic, but very bubbly and satisfying. $23.

Dessert Wine

BEDELL EIS
As in the German eiswein, or ice wine. The dessert wine is primarily riesling and invariably alluring. Dried fruits define it. And you won't be overtaken by sweetness; indeed, there's a touch of tartness and firmness in there that contrasts with and complements the lush, honey qualities. Excellent. Half bottle, $27.

1995 DUCK WALK APHRODITE
The Greek goddess of love lends her name to this late-harvest gewürztraminer. The wine includes some riesling. Honeysuckle, peach notes. But not very deep. $28. Half bottle, $15.

1994 DUCK WALK APHRODITE
The wine hints of apricot, sometimes peach. Balanced, bright. Have it very chilled. $22. Half-bottle, $12.

1996 JAMESPORT LATE HARVEST RIESLING
A winning wine, honeyed, ripe and attractive, with suggestions of apricot. Concentrated flavors. One of the winery's best. Half-bottle, $25.

1996 PALMER SELECT LATE HARVEST GEWÜRZTRAMINER

Compared with the 1994, this wine is lighter and crisper. That's courtesy of a cool end to the season. But an attractive, perfumed wine. Half-bottle, $16.

1994 PALMER SELECT LATE HARVEST GEWÜRZTRAMINER

Superb. Wonderfully ripe, honeyed, aromatic, full of peach, with a trace of spice and a rare richness. Exceptional expression of the style. Half bottle, $25.

1997 PAUMANOK LATE HARVEST RIESLING

Paumanok's elegant, rosy and very ripe dessert wine is full of fruit, luscious and celebratory on its own: a marvelous way to conclude your dinner, or to have a treat. Half bottle, $19.

1997 PAUMANOK LATE HARVEST SAUVIGNON BLANC

Ripe and grand, one of the best dessert wines ever made on Long Island. It has good acidity and distinctive character. A lush and seductive evocation of France, superb at meal's end or anytime, really. Look for it. Half bottle, $29.

1994 PAUMANOK LATE HARVEST SAUVIGNON BLANC

Lovely dessert wine, with an elegant sweetness that doesn't overwhelm the flavors of apricot and peach. It will remind you of a Sauternes. Long finish. Half bottle, $25.

1994 PAUMANOK SELECT LATE HARVEST RIESLING

A fruity, accessible dessert wine, with the character of dried apricot. Very flavorful, with few demands. Half bottle, $13

1993 PAUMANOK LATE HARVEST RIESLING

Honeyed, with excellent fruit. Still fine, though hard to locate. Half bottle, $15.

1994 PECONIC BAY LATE HARVEST RIESLING

A deft dessert wine, heady with the flavor of apricot, and honey on the finish. The wine has traces of sweet spiciness to it. Light and fruity, very enjoyable. Half bottle, $13.

1996 PELLEGRINI FINALE

Not much of this attractive dessert wine was made. The alluring sweet wine is 70 percent gewürztraminer and 30 percent sauvignon blanc. Hints of orange peel. It has a lovely finish. Half bottle, $25.

1995 PELLEGRINI FINALE

Excellent, layered, honeyed, ripe dessert wine, with good acidity and fresh mouthfeel. As refreshing as it is lush on the palate, with intensifying aspects of golden raisins, litchis, apricots. Holding up nicely. Half bottle, $25.

1994 PELLEGRINI FINALE

Lots of honeyed richness mark this edition of Finale, which is 70 percent gewürztraminer and 30 percent riesling. It's also a fruitier version of the wine, high-octane and seductive, but not recklessly sweet. Fine with cheeses or solo. Half bottle, $25.

1993 PELLEGRINI FINALE

The '93 production is 73 percent gewürztraminer and 27 percent sauvignon blanc. Local "ice wine." It could use more acid. The wine was aged 14 months in oak. The flavor suggests golden raisins and apricots. Have it with cheeses such as Roquefort and Gorgonzola, or with pears. $48. Half bottle, $25.

1996 PINDAR JOHANNISBERG RIESLING

Here's Pindar's big sweet at meal's end: an ice wine with a flourish. Brix, 31; residual sugar, 18. Have it slightly chilled and enjoy a treat. The temptation is to consume the wine with a dessert, but it is really best tasted on its own. Half bottle, $35.

1995 PUGLIESE LATE HARVEST NIAGARA

The grape of the Finger Lakes visits Long Island, with just so-so results. The very grapey, sweetish white has a fadeaway quality. More an engaging experiment. Half bottle, $10.

Port

1996 DUCK WALK BLUEBERRY PORT

This could just as easily be listed in the next category. A curiosity, for sure, made from wild Maine blueberries. Not much to it. Half bottle, $13.

OSPREY'S DOMINION PORT

Sleekly dressed, this nonvintage Port is a warming number made from cabernet sauvignon. Not utterly smooth. $10.

1994 PINDAR CABERNET PORT

Bracing and warming, the '94 Port is made from 100 percent cabernet sauvignon. Well-fortified, but with soft tannins. Satisfactory with cheese. Half bottle, $13.

1992 PINDAR CABERNET PORT

To take the chill off any evening, you can warm up with this gutsy creation. Not Fonseca, but respectable stuff and done with the winery's customary vigor. Bracing, quite sweet. It should be in shape for several years. $23. Half bottle $13.

1996 PUGLIESE WHITE PORT

Made mainly with Niagara grapes. A sweet and fruity experiment, this wine is always in short supply. $15.

1994 PUGLIESE PORT BELLO

A luscious, warming, wood-aged port made primarily from cabernet sauvignon and merlot. It doesn't compare with the real thing, in part because of the grapes that are used. But bello. $15.

Something Different

BEDELL RASPBERRY WINE
Very sweet, aromatic and high-octane, it's made with fermented raspberry juice that's fortified with distilled grape juice. A potent combo. Serve it slightly chilled. Or cook with it. Half bottle, $10.

DUCK WALK BOYSENBERRY DESSERT WINE
Sundae topping. Better for cooking than drinking. Half bottle, $13.

OSPREY'S DOMINION SPICE WINE
A rescue mission for wine that wasn't ideal for release, this spiced wine can be microwaved without damaging it. The beverage contains cinnamon, nutmeg and clove, which were steeped like a tea bag. A local version of glogg, the Swedish spin on mulled wine. $9.

OSPREY'S DOMINION STRAWBERRY WINE
Colorful and fun, whether on its own, as a mixer, a spritzer, a mock-kir. Goes with vodka, too. Snobs will die. $9.

CHAPTER 6

Vine to Wine

The process explained

For all its mysteries and romance, winemaking starts as farming. It begins with the soil. The elegant and symbolic vine is, finally, a tree with fruit. You plant it and go on from there.

What makes the difference between an outstanding wine and a candidate for vinegar are the decision-making and the details; the specific grape variety, the precise location and type of soil, the exact climate.

Which explains why Alex and Louisa Hargrave pioneered winemaking on the North Fork instead of in North Dakota.

"The soil is sandy loam and well-drained, and the roots don't get choked in clay," said Alex Hargrave, who explored locations as far afield as Oregon before planting in Cutchogue. "You can't imagine how hard it is to work in the Finger Lakes" because of the hard soil and the shorter growing season.

The "microclimate" of the North Fork results in a season that's considerably longer than upstate's. The region is well-suited for red varietals such as merlot and cabernet franc.

The South Fork is cooler, and generally more conducive to white wine grapes, though in recent vintages there have been notable reds.

Unusual local conditions, from the altitude of a vineyard to the effects of an ocean breeze, can spur grapes in unlikely areas. "We have a series of undulations running through the vineyard, and a variety of soil types and exposures," said Russell Hearn, winemaker at Pellegrini Vineyards in Cutchogue. "Cabernet sauvignon should be on well-drained, sandier sites. Chardonnay or merlot can handle heavier soil types."

What matters even more than the composition of the soil and the rock, is its capacity for drainage and water storage, so the roots have a reliable supply. Winemakers need to know a little geology before getting into chemistry and microbiology.

Once they determine that a stretch of land will produce ripe grapes regularly, they may find that one part of the vineyard is very different from another. One side of a hill, one lot, one block, will be different from another. Sloping land allows for warmer temperatures at the upper end. And the amount of sunlight and winds may not be the same throughout the vineyard. The union of soil and climate often does make wine from the same grape variety differ from region to region. All merlots aren't identical.

Wine starts as a branch, or shoot, of a grapevine. It's cut and planted. Leaves and roots grow. It becomes a rootstock, a hardy branch of grapevine. The rootstock is selected for its strength. Growers acquire rootstocks, and cuttings of wine-producing vines are grafted onto them. These cuttings establish the grape variety.

Vitis vinifera is the native European species that yields the top wines, from chardonnay and riesling to cabernet sauvignon and pinot noir. Long Island is New York State's prime region for *Vitis vinifera*. Hybrids such as concord and catawba, seyval blanc and baco noir are more suited for the colder weather upstate.

Vinifera is hardy, too. But more than a century ago, vineyards in France were ruined by phylloxera, a louse from native American plants that dined on vinifera roots. Phylloxera also wiped out California vineyards in the 1880s. Some native American species resisted phylloxera, however, and an effective way to combat the louse was found: grafting vinifera onto rootstock with the immunity. Most wine-producing vines now are the result of this marriage.

Rootstocks are planted in spring. Grafting is summertime work. By the following spring, there should be growth from the grafted bud. The plant is trimmed and protected to ensure growth of the bud and direct the growth upward.

Depending on the location, three to seven years will pass before the vineyard produces a harvestable crop from those vines. Each grapevine has its own cycle for maturation.

Winemakers use "canopy management," or trimming of the vine into its most effective shape. There are several methods of pruning and training a vine. The systems are geared to spread leaves and, accordingly, cut back shade and capture sunlight. What's used depends on the grape. Vinifera grapes have "an upright growth habit," said Louisa Hargrave. "Hybrids drape downward."

The Fruit's the Thing

To make excellent wine, you need excellent fruit. "It is the most crucial component," said Charles Massoud of Paumanok Vineyards in Aquebogue. "The old phrase is 'The wine is made in the vineyard, not in the winery.' If you don't make mistakes, you can make very good wine. But you're not going to be able to improve on the quality of the fruit."

The grape on the vine ripens in stages.

Basically, the grape becomes larger and heavier, accumulates sugars, reduces acids, forms its tannins and aromas, and changes skin color.

Each type of grape, depending on climate, has a particular time to be picked. Chardonnay is early; cabernet sauvignon, late. Long Island requires an unusually long and sunny stretch to produce first-rate cabernet sauvignon. An earlier-ripening red, such as merlot, has an advantage on the North and South Forks.

From the time the berries form until ripening begins is the opening act. Ripening starts, the fruit swells, and the colors change. White grapes go from green to yellow; and black grapes from green to light red and then dark red. The sugar in the grapes rises quickly.

That's followed by ripening to full maturity, as the grape continues to swell, heighten its sugar and lose acidity. There are times when the grape stays on the vine beyond maturation. The overripe grape, a source of dessert wines, is more concentrated in sugar.

Harvesting starts when the winemaker decides that the correct ratio of acid and sugar in the grapes has been achieved. A grape can offer different degrees of tartness and sweetness. It will gain sugar through photosynthesis during a sunny growing season, such as in 1995 and 1997 on Long Island. Without sufficient sun and heat, grapes won't ripen properly and the wines won't be as good. Maximum ripeness is the goal and the grapes are monitored every day.

Grapes are harvested primarily by machine. But some producers continue to harvest by hand, especially for dessert wines. Sometimes, grapes are harvested when frozen, for sweet "ice wine." On Long Island, ice wines are from grapes that are frozen commercially.

Crushing and Pressing

When the harvested grapes rest on each other, they produce free-run juice, or juice without machine pressing. The crush and the press follow. The crush part of the process involves removing stems and breaking skins, releasing the pulp, allowing the juices to flow. The crusher and destemmer are similar to a strainer, with paddles separating grapes and stems.

Pressing has become a gentler process than it used to be. For white wines, skins and juice are separated in the presser. If the skins and juice aren't separated immediately, the skin may impart additional flavor to white wines. For rosé wine, the juice has slight contact with the dark skins.

To make red wine, the juice, skins, pulp and seeds are piped into fermentation tanks. Red wine stays with the skins through fermentation and occasionally beyond. That gives the wine color. The skins have phenolics, compounds that can make the wine astringent. Fermentation containers are stainless-steel temperature-controlled tanks or oak barrels.

Grapes develop natural yeasts. They may be airborne in the vineyard and on the bloom on the grape's skin. Yeast contacts the sugars in the juice, and the sugars are converted to alcohol and carbon dioxide.

Winemakers add selected strains of cultured yeast to the mixture because natural yeasts may be inconsistent. The special yeasts bring a particular quality to the wine, such as aromatics.

The fermenting juice is monitored constantly, until the sugar has been transformed to alcohol. A hydrometer is used to measure the decreasing sugar. The alcohol level goes up. The yeasts perish. Coolants in the steel tanks regulate temperatures, enabling the producer to control the fermentation rate.

In still wines, the carbon dioxide goes into the air; for sparkling wines, the carbon dioxide stays in. Most of the sparklers are made via a second fermentation, in tank or bottle. A sugar-yeast combination is added to do it.

During red-wine fermentation, skins and seeds bubble to the surface. The resulting "cap" is punched down manually or from a stream of juice pumped up from the tank's bottom.

If the winery is producing a fortified wine, such as Port, fermentation is halted when neutral spirits are added. This jars the yeasts while the wine still is sweet to increase the alcohol.

After fermentation for still wine, a process that can last weeks, comes clarification, letting the wine settle and transferring it to another barrel or tank. The goal is to remove solids. The longer the wine can be left to settle, the less maneuvering has to occur later.

Sediment, mostly from the yeast, is called the "lees." Some wines intentionally are given more contact with the lees to heighten flavor.

After Fermentation, Fine Tuning

Malolactic fermentation is a secondary fermentation for reds and some whites to soften the wine. It converts the assertive malic acid to weaker lactic acid and carbon dioxide. This fermentation is considered helpful when there's too much acidity.

Chaptalization is another action used to shape wine in cooler climates. Sugar is added to make up for underripe grapes and thereby produce more alcohol. In warmer regions, tartaric acid may be added to compensate for lower natural acidity.

The wine also may be filtered before bottling, by passing it through ducts or pores that act as strainers and isolate particles. But not all wines are filtered. Fining, using a substance such as beaten egg whites or gelatins to attract solids, is a technique to clarify wine, too.

Some wines will age, some will go to the bottling line. White wines typically are bottled within a year. Red wines usually aren't. The winemaker decides how long to keep the wine in the tanks or the oak barrels. Every winery has its approach with each wine and each vintage. It can be weeks or years.

"This is three different businesses," said Joel Lauber, co-owner of Corey Creek Vineyards in Southold. "You have to grow the fruit, and you can fail there easily. Then, you have to make decent wine. Then you have to market it.

"And you can't do it two-out-of-three."

CHAPTER 7

The Match Game

Which wine with that fish?

R ed or white? It's a question to make you blush.
There have been essays, tracts, and books
written about whether it's criminal to serve a
fish with red wine or beef with white. History doubt-
less records wars of the rosés, too.

The main thing to keep in mind is whether you
like the flavor that results. Wine and food have their
own specific tastes; when they come together, a third
is created.

Also, whether you're thinking about poaching a
salmon or opening a can of tuna, remember that
whatever sauce or dressing ends up on the entree can
have more impact on the appropriateness of the wine
you drink than the properties of the main ingredient
itself.

All this inevitably leads to shorthand, if only to
make pairings easier. And any quick reference,
whether it's a star rating for a restaurant or a
"thumb's up" for a movie, can be seen as strict cod-
ification. So, it's best to view charts and ratings as
general references, not precise directives.

There is no meal that calls for a solitary, perfect
wine. The perfect wine is a product of the imagina-
tion, not the chef. Plenty of different wines are terrific with plenty of different dishes.

It's also true, however, that some foods have a
head-on run-in with some wines. You wouldn't want

to have spicy, upfront barbecue with a mild white; or subtle sole in butter sauce with a big, tannic red. Have a few walnuts, which are tannic in themselves, with an astringent wine, such as an immature cabernet sauvignon, and you'll definitely pucker up, though not in the romantic way.

The most sensible way to think about matching food and wine is straightforward. Decide on the body and the texture of the food and of the wine, and the flavors. For example:

Consider whether the dish is salty or sweet, rich or not. Or whether it's highly spiced, awash in cream sauce, smoky, peppery, plain. Then, figure whether you want what's in the glass to be similar or to contrast with what's on the plate.

If you're planning a multi-course meal with several wines, the traditional approach is to serve wines that are lighter in body and less complicated in taste before heavyweight, complex wines. White wines precede reds. Dry wines arrive before sweet ones. Young is drunk before old. And you can enjoy a light red before a full-bodied white without causing an international crisis.

You don't have to uncork a different bottle with every course. A lot of meals go well with just a white wine, or a red or a rosé. Certain wines do have an all-purpose role, and that accounts in part for their popularity. Beaujolais, the fruity red, is a dependable bottle on the wine list. Accessible, soft merlot has soared because of its easy-drinking quality and versatility. Pinot grigio does the same for whites, along with sauvignon blanc and some rieslings. Champagne and other sparkling wines are festive and excellent before you get to the appetizers.

Friends and Enemies

But all wines don't harmonize with all foods. If you drank an acidic wine with a vinegary salad, the taste would be wiped out. Fruit vinegars, however, may not do the same. Sparkling wine combats saltiness. Mayonnaise and chocolates upend wine. It has been argued for years that an artichoke can wreck wine. Biochemistry is cited. To which the equally acceptable replies may be quiet agreement or "So what?"

It is known that protein helps break down tannin, the preservative compound in grape skins that gives red wine astringency and a longer life. It follows that a steak tastes great with a full-bodied cabernet sauvignon.

Milk also has protein that lessens the tannin in red wine. This is one of the reasons why cheese so readily goes with red wine. And why you can have a cheeseburger with your favorite red, too. High tannin and acidity help cut the richness of a dish.

Wine and food matches that at first might not seem sensible can turn out to be memorable. At the pricey end, devotees of recklessly rich foie gras will find a ripe partner with the elegant sweetness of Sauternes. If you're into the third or fourth shared dish at a Chinese feast, the aromatic and floral qualities of gewürztraminer will contentedly take part.

Seafood and lamb are among the entrees-in-waiting that call for contrasts. When preparing seafood, you'll note that what's first-rate with fish in cream sauce will not be with grilled fish. And what appears flawless with delicate, firm Dover sole won't necessarily be perfect with oily bluefish. The wine that has an affinity with lightly sauced salmon may not be enamored with the smoked variety. Seasoning can mask the primary characteristics of dish, whether fish or meat.

The compatibility between foods and wines stems from geography, too. When you sample the deep flavors and wintry cooking of Piedmontese cuisine, it's not surprising to see that Barolos and Barbarescos are apropos.

For the lighter foods of this region of northern Italy, a dolcetto is a mainstay. Similarly, choucroute, the soulful combination of sauerkraut and pork, naturally links up with an Alsatian riesling. And paella marries well with Rioja.

On Long Island, the local merlots and duckling are a popular pairing. So are the lobsters and the chardonnays.

Red or white?

Following are some suggestions for matching wines and foods. The wines aren't limited to those produced on Long Island. But all are available here.

Antipasti
pinot grigio, Orvieto, dolcetto, Barbera

Artichokes
sauvignon/fumé blanc

Asparagus
riesling, chenin blanc

Barbecue
zinfandel, shiraz, Barbera

Roast beef
cabernet sauvignon, merlot, zinfandel

Beef brisket
cabernet sauvignon

Beef stew
cabernet sauvignon, Rhône Valley reds

Bluefish
light merlot, sauvignon/fumé blanc

Caesar salad
sauvignon/fumé blanc

Cajun dishes
sauvignon/fumé blanc, gamay, Beaujolais

Carpaccio
light reds

Caviar
sparkling wine

Chicken pot pie
riesling, pinot blanc

Fried chicken
light chardonnay, gamay, Beaujolais

Grilled chicken
chardonnay, Chianti, merlot

Roast chicken
light merlot, gamay

Chili
zinfandel, rosé, gamay

Chinese dishes
sauvignon/fume blanc, gewürztraminer, riesling

Fried clams
light chardonnay

Raw clams
pinot grigio

Cod
chardonnay

Cold cuts
fruity reds, rosé

Crab cakes
sauvignon/fumé blanc, dry riesling

Soft-shell crab
sauvignon/fumé blanc, pinot blanc

Curry
gewürztraminer, sauvignon/fumé blanc

Roast duck
cabernet sauvignon, merlot, pinot noir, zinfandel

Duck with fruit sauce
chardonnay, zinfandel

Eggs
fruity whites, light reds

Eggplant Parmigiana
Chianti, dolcetto

Filet mignon
merlot, red Burgundy

Fish and chips
sauvignon/fumé blanc

Fish stew
pinot blanc, rosé, light merlot

Flounder
chardonnay, pinot blanc, sauvignon/fumé blanc

Foie gras
Sauternes, late-harvest sauvignon/fumé blanc

Game
Barolo, red Burgundy, Rhône reds, zinfandel, pinot noir

Greek dishes
sauvignon/fumé blanc

Halibut
chardonnay, pinot grigio

Ham
fruity riesling, rosés, light chardonnay

Hamburgers
zinfandel, merlot, Chianti

Hot dogs
Beaujolais, gamay, fruity riesling

Indian dishes
gewürztraminer, gamay

Japanese dishes
light chardonnay, chenin blanc, sauvignon/fumé blanc

Lasagna
Chianti, Barbera, merlot

Liver
cabernet sauvignon, merlot

Meat loaf
zinfandel, merlot

Roast lamb
red Bordeaux, cabernet sauvignon,

merlot, zinfandel

Baked/stuffed lobster
chardonnay, sauvignon/fumé blanc

Broiled lobster
chardonnay, sparkling wine

Steamed lobster
white Burgundies, chardonnay

Mexican dishes
fruity whites and reds, rosé

Monkfish
chardonnay

Mushrooms
Chianti, Barolo, merlot

Steamed mussels
pinot blanc, blanc, chardonnay

Onion soup
Beaujolais, gamay

Oysters
Chablis, Sancerre, sauvignon/fumé blanc

Paella
red or white Rioja

Pasta with cream sauce
chardonnay

Pasta with seafood/ red sauce
light merlot

Pasta with seafood/ white sauce
Verdicchio, pinot grigio, light chardonnay

Pasta with meat sauce
Barbera, Chianti, dolcetto, merlot

Pasta with pesto
chardonnay

Pasta with tomato sauce
cabernet franc, Barbera

Pasta with vegetables
fruity whites

Stuffed peppers
rosé, light reds

Pizza
Chianti, shiraz, red Rioja, merlot

Pork chops
chardonnay, merlot

Roast pork
riesling, light reds

Pot roast
zinfandel, Beaujolais

Porterhouse steak
cabernet sauvignon, zinfandel, shiraz

Prime rib
cabernet sauvignon, Rhône reds

Quiche
pinot blanc, riesling

Rabbit
merlot, cabernet franc

Grilled salmon
chardonnay, rosé, merlot, pinot noir

Poached salmon
sauvignon/fumé blanc, riesling

Scallops
gewürztraminer, fruity riesling, sauvignon/fumé blanc

Shrimp cocktail
chenin blanc, pinot blanc

Grilled shrimp
sauvignon/fumé blanc

Sirloin steak
cabernet sauvignon, merlot, Barolo

Smoked fish
Sancerre, gewürztraminer, muscat, sauvignon/fume blanc

Snapper
sauvignon/fumé blanc, chardonnay

Sole
pinot blanc, sauvignon/fumé blanc, chenin blanc

Striped bass
chardonnay

Sushi
chenin blanc, riesling, gewürztraminer

Swordfish
chardonnay, light reds

Thai dishes
chenin blanc, pinot grigio, rosé, light merlot

Trout
riesling, light whites

Tuna
fruity whites, merlot

Turkey
dry riesling, pinot noir, zinfandel, light red Burgundy

Roast veal
chardonnay, sauvignon/fumé blanc, pinot noir

Veal chops
cabernet sauvignon, merlot

Veal piccata
pinot blanc, sauvignon/fumé blanc

Venison
cabernet sauvignon, Rhône reds, Barolo, zinfandel

Vietnamese dishes
gewürztraminer, rosé

CHAPTER 8

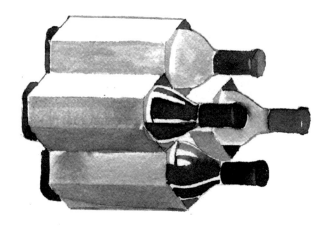

Swirl, Sniff, Spit...

Tasting is detective work

Wine tastings could make you spit. Then again, that's something you have to do, unless you want to turn horizontal at a vertical tasting. There's a difference between wine tasting and wine swallowing.

And there are reasons for all that sniffing and swirling.

You're gathering information, finding how a good wine reveals itself and what qualities it possesses. It can be both entertaining and educational.

There are different kinds of tastings. In a horizontal tasting, you sample wines of the same vintage from different producers; for example, a dozen Long Island merlots from 1993. A vertical tasting compares different vintages of the same wine; for example, Lenz Merlot, from 1988 to 1995.

An enjoyable and lighthearted introductory tasting could bring together different grape varieties, or the same grapes from different regions, allowing you to determine similarities and differences.

For example, you could sample a chardonnay, a riesling, a gewürztraminer, and a sauvignon blanc; or, a cabernet sauvignon, a pinot noir, a merlot and a gamay.

Then, examine chardonnays only, from Burgundy, California, Australia and Italy; or merlots from

California, Pomerol or Saint-Emilion, Washington State and Long Island.

Of course, you don't have to go through all the formalities of a tasting to enjoy wine. And you shouldn't bother applying those techniques to wines that are routine. Consider six general categories for white wines and four for reds, along with one for fortified wines, higher-alcohol wines to which spirits have been added.

Styles of Wine

Aromatic white wines
These wines have floral, fruity and herbal qualities. They include muscat, sauvignon/fumé blanc, gewürztraminer, pinot grigio and some German riesling. ness. They're very appealing, light, and pair well with food. Good on their own, too. Johannisberg riesling, chenin blanc, Müller-Thurgau, gray riesling and Vouvray are indicative.

Light, dry white wines
They're mild wines, and could be seen as all-purpose. You may enjoy them as aperitifs, with a variety of foods, or for a casual drink. Among these wines are pinot blanc, Verdicchio, Orvieto, Muscadet and some Chablis.

Medium-bodied, dry white wines
Such wines have more varietal character: you know you're drinking a chardonnay or a riesling. Some of these are Chablis, Chassagne-Montrachet, U.S. chardonnays, Alsatian riesling, and Greco di Tufo.

Full-bodied, dry white wines
The wines have more complexity, greater texture. The great whites such as Le Montrachet and Corton-Charlemagne are examples, as are Meursault, Graves and top U.S. chardonnays.

Fruity, off-dry whites
These display some sweet-

Sweet
Dessert wines, with the ultimate ripeness of the fruit, and high sugar content. Trockenbeerenauslese and Beerenauslese from Germany, Sauternes and Barsac from France, ice wines, and late-harvest U.S. varietals.

Light, fruity red wines
They're young and have a grapey quality. Tannin is low. Beaujolais and Beaujolais Nouveau are typical. Also dolcetto, gamay, Grenache and Valpolicella.

Medium-bodied, dry red wines
These display more varietal character and texture. Merlot, cabernet franc, Chianti Classico, Côtes-du-Rhône, some Burgundies and some U.S. cabernet sauvignon fit the description.

Full-bodied, dry red wines
They have deeper flavors and more texture. For full-bodied,

dry reds, consider syrah/shiraz, zinfandel, some Rioja wines, some Bordeaux and Burgundies, and certain U.S. cabernet sauvignon.

Big, powerful, dry red wines

Here are the long-lived, rich, tannic and complex wines. The top Bordeaux and Burgundies, Côte-Rôtie and Hermitage also from France, Barolo and Brunello di Montalcino from Italy.

Fortified wines

A fortified wine results when brandy or neutral spirits are added to increase the wine's alcohol content. Some fortified wines have more than 20 per cent alcohol, compared with between 7 and 14 per cent for dry, table wine. Fortified wines include Port, Sherry, Madeira, Málaga and Marsala.

It's Your Call

In tasting these and other wines, what matters is whether you like the wine and are curious about what attracts you, not whether your opinion coincides with that of veteran tasters.

Nothing affects anyone's viewpoint, professional or amateur, more than seeing the label. So, hold a blind tasting, which will allow for better judgment. And it pays to do your tasting in a place with lighting that won't distort the colors of the wine. There shouldn't be any foreign odors either, whether from food or cigarette smoke. They'll alter your ability to smell the wine.

By the way, if you have a cold, postpone the tasting.

That's because so much of wine tasting actually is what you smell. Your palate is limited to sweet, sour, salty and bitter. But through the nose, you encounter thousands of aromas and flavors.

First, however, you ought to look at the wine to judge its clarity and texture. Wine should be bright and clear. Ideally it will have been poured into a thin, colorless, stemmed glass with a bowl that narrows at the rim. Such a glass will let you see the wine best, and will concentrate the aromas. A couple of ounces is enough.

Look into the glass from overhead and check the wine's color depth. Tilt your glass away, preferably against a white background. The action spreads the wine and enables you to observe color and viscosity — whether it's thin and watery, or heavy — determined by how its film adheres to the sides of the glass. A light white wine won't have the texture of a honey-like dessert wine.

With white wines, you'll see a range of colors that go from pale yellow-green through straw to deeper yellow to deep gold. Or to brown, if the wine has gone bad.

With red wines, the colors move from purplish and ruby to brick red, to almost black. A little brown indicates the wine is older. Full-blown brown, however, isn't good for a red, either. It signals the wine is shot.

The colors indicate age and grape variety, important information about the wine you'll taste. They will help distinguish one wine from another. A young Beaujolais will have a purple shade; a vintage red Bordeaux will be brick red, with a tinge of mahogany on the edge. A great dessert wine such as a peak Sauternes becomes golden. Compare that with a very light German or Italian white, or a pale Graves.

Using Your Nose

Now, to the sniffing, which unveils many of the specific characteristics of the wine. Much of this is free association more than the application of rigorous criteria.

Take a whiff just after the wine is poured. Then swirl the wine and sniff again. You may get two different sensations. The swirling lets more oxygen get to the wine. And that aeration intensifies the smell, the aroma of the grape variety, the bouquet developed in the winemaking.

It spurs the release of those molecules of flavor on the surface. Vapors rise. Inhale. You're bringing the wine in contact, eventually, with the olfactory bulb. That's where the sensations make their impression. The wine is stimulating nerve cells.

You'll tell the difference quickly between, for example, a very fragrant riesling or a gewürztraminer, and a chardonnay. Or between a plummy merlot and a spicy zinfandel.

Countless scents are found in wines. Professors at the University of California at Davis developed an "aroma wheel" that attempts to organize many of them, from earthy, fruity, chemical, floral, spicy and vegetative into more precise divisions, such as the type of fruit and the sort of flower.

In a red wine such as a Long Island merlot, you're apt to discover the fruity aromas of plum and berries; in cabernet sauvignon, perhaps cassis and cherries.

For a white wine such as a chardonnay, the fruity qualities may be pear, green apple or pineapple; for riesling, peach and apricot; gewürztraminer, litchi; and sauvignon blanc, lemon and grapefruit.

Sip the wine, letting some air in over it. Judge how the wine feels in the mouth. Slosh it around the palate. Swallow a bit. Then, exhale a little with nose and mouth. You'll learn how long the wine lingers.

Your tongue's tip detects sweetness; the middle, the fruit and tannin; the sides, acidity. You'll find whether the wine is soft or harsh, see whether the flavors are sustained, and gather impressions of the texture and the finish.

A chardonnay may suggest vanilla or butteriness; cabernet sauvignon, mint; zinfandel, black pepper; pinot noir, earthiness, as in mushrooms.

You'll be sure whether the wine is sweet or dry, acidic or tannic, balanced or not. And you can start using terms like "crisp" for acidity or "flabby" for lack of it. Or skip the vocabulary part.

Drink or Hold

Wine is alive. You can enjoy its company young. You can grow old with it. Or you can kill it. And there are a lot of ways to commit vinicide.

Actually, the best place to allow wine to age is a lot like a tomb: dark, cool and slightly damp. But more wine drinkers have hall closets than stone cellars.

Besides, most wines are made to be drunk earlier than later, if not immediately. Fruity, lighter wines are very popular, in part because the wine is ready to drink once it's bottled. And the wine usually is consumed soon after purchase. Long Island wines are no exception, even though a number of the reds have a decade or more of life in them.

So, unless you keep a bottle upright in the sun atop your boiler, it will likely survive until you drink it.

But if you plan to store a good bottle beyond beyond six months to a year, you should think about where it ought to be, apart from within reach.

Wine's biggest enemies are heat, light, turbulence. Basically, you don't want to stash your best in the back seat of the car en route to a July Florida vacation while the kids are trying to poke a hole in the cork. The wine reacts to each stimulus.

Great wines age and mature well when they're stored on their sides at a temperature of 50 to 59 degrees Fahrenheit, with proper humidity, shielded from the sun that nurtured the grapes.

Wine is perishable. It's not wise, however, to put a bottle in your refrigerator for years. The maturing of wine can be retarded when it's resting place is too cold. Drop the temperature into the mid-20s, and lighter wines could get frosty.

If the spot is too warm, you'll be unintentionally speeding up the wine's life, but not improving it. Light also ages a wine prematurely. If the wine is in an environment pushing 80 degrees, the volatile compounds in the wine will be murdered, cooked away.

Overall, the temperature in the wine space shouldn't vary by more than about 20 degrees. Major changes in temperature can wreck wine. And if it's not humid enough, the cork eventually will dry, allowing air to spoil the wine.

The reason wines are stored on their sides is to keep the cork moist and swollen, acting as a seal. Also, the bottle's neck is filled, so oxygen doesn't go in. Oxygen will ruin the wine. You also could angle the bottle to allow both the wine and the air bubble to touch the cork, leaving room for any expansion that occurs if the temperature changes significantly.

This applies to all wines in bottles with corks. Even Beaujolais Nouveau may benefit from a few months of proper storage. But the major goal is to let potentially long-lived wines mature steadily at their own pace, free from factors that either slow or speed the process.

There's no way to make wine develop quickly. You pay more for wines that have aging potential. So, it makes sense to treat them carefully.

Storage Options

Racks and bins are the most common ways to store wine at home. If you have a house with a basement, the below-ground locale probably is your storage area. A dark closet also works. Pigeonhole systems, with a space for each bottle, and stacking systems in diamond-shaped bins are the most familiar.

Or, you could keep the wine in the producer's wooden or cardboard cases. But the humidity that nurtures the wine may cause cardboard to give way and wood to develop mold.

Temperature and humidity-controlled cabinets are increasingly popular, as interest in wine has grown and disposable income among buyers has risen. These units, which look like refrigerators, vary widely in size and price. They do provide the right conditions when nature doesn't. You're above-ground, too.

At Kedco Wine Storage in Farmingdale, the cost of these typically begins at about $400 for a 24-bottle unit. A 700-bottle unit is about $3,000. Installing prefabricated rooms and converting existing rooms to wine cellars are among the company's projects, too.

If you're keeping fewer than 24 wines and plan to drink them within the next few months, you probably don't need an appliance-type unit. Stack the wine, and leave a bowl of water for humidity nearby.

At the other extreme, if you've got 1,000 bottles rolling around, some kind of orderly system will help. At least you'll be able to find the bottle you want.

An alternative: a company such as Wine Services, Inc. in Riverhead rents space in a temperature-and-humidity-controlled storage facility.

Long Live the Wine!

Wines that have long lives frequently are expensive. They're typically the tannic and concentrated reds. Long Island wines that are expected to last longer are red blends, such as Pindar's Mythology, Pellegrini's Encore, Paumanok's Assemblage, and Palmer's Select Reserve; and merlots and cabernet sauvignons from years such as 1993 and 1995.

But since the industry is comparatively young, wines from the mid-1980s are considered the senior class. Some reds from that period are drinking well now, and have the potential to mature even more. Bedell's 1988 Reserve Merlot and Gristina's 1988 Cabernet Sauvignon are examples.

The top red Bordeaux have the most impressive record for longevity. Some can mature for 50 years or more. From a high-quality vintage, expect red Bordeaux to last at least 20 years.

Stellar red Burgundies, such as those from Romanée-Conti, Musigny, and Chambertin, are generally more in the 15-year span. A Rhône star such as Côte-Rôtie or Hermitage may go a little longer. And the grand Italian reds such as Barolo, Barbaresco and Brunello di Montalcino go 20-plus years.

Cabernet sauvignon from California has shown aging potential, from producers such as Heitz and Mondavi. But the wineries are quite young.

White wines that last are the peak white Burgundies, such as Le Montrachet and Corton-Charlemagne. Dessert wines, from late-harvest German rieslings to Sauternes, age beautifully. So do the premier Champagnes, such as Moët & Chandon's Dom Perignon and Veuve Clicquot's La Grande Dame, and the best from Salon, Krug and Bollinger. Vintage Ports, from makers such as Fonseca, Taylor, and Quinta do Noval are known for their longevity.

Wine collecting itself is a hobby. What it's collected in is akin to a booklover's shelves or a cigar smoker's humidor. You choose which items deserve the friendly confines as opposed to the exile of inattention.

If the bottle has a screw cap, don't worry about it.

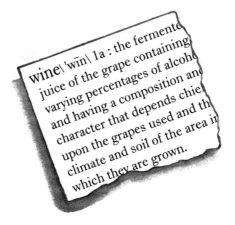

wine\ˈwīn\ 1a : the fermented
juice of the grape containing
varying percentages of alcohol
and having a composition and
character that depends chiefly
upon the grapes used and the
climate and soil of the area in
which they are grown.

What Are They Talking About?

A guide to winespeak

Trying to understand wine tasters at work can be similar to deconstructing dialogues on the upper levels of the Tower of Babel. It could lead you to drink.

The conversation starts getting strange when you find yourself among people describing wine the way you'd talk about a local politician: "dumb," "backward," "foxy," "flabby."

Philosophers of language may spend years on the topic. But you want to know whether the wine is any good.

I've tried to avoid the jargon of wine writing in this book. Some technical terms, however, are in the text. What follows is a brief guide to winespeak.

Acetic — Vinegary. Not a good quality in taste or smell for any wine.

Acidity — How much acid is in a wine. From malic, tartaric and citric acid. Tartaric acid leads to the crisp flavor of some wines; malic, some

fruitiness; citric, less. Other acids are produced in fermentation, too. As a wine ages, acidity dips.

Aging — In barrels, casks or bottles, this allows the wine time to improve. Aging often imparts a desired taste. The great red wines usually need aging to reach their peak. But most wines, especially whites, are ready to drink when they're released.

Aeration — Allowing air to reach the wine. You can do this by swirling it in a glass, or by decanting the wine, pouring it from the bottle into another container.

American Viticultural Area — Or, AVA. It's a system of identification of U.S. wines by geography. Eighty-five per cent of the grapes must be grown in the area to receive the designation. On Long Island, the Hamptons and the North Fork are separate viticultural areas.

Ampelography — It's the word for the classification and study of grape varieties.

Angular — Used to describe young wines leaving a tart impression. Naturally, it means the wine isn't round.

Appley — Used in describing the aroma of a wine. Typical scents are green apple, which suggests young grapes; or ripe apple.

Aroma — The fragrance of the wine that's from the fruit. Typically, it will suggest either specific fruits or flowers, but also the wine's particular varietal characteristics and developments during fermentation and aging. Different from bouquet.

Austere — Short on fruit, due either to the compounds known as tannins or to acid.

Backward — An undeveloped wine.

Balance — A goal of winemakers is harmony, so that none of the qualities of a wine, from fruit to tannin, sweetness to acidity, outweighs the others. In a balanced wine, the aroma wouldn't be stronger than the taste; the taste wouldn't wipe out the aroma.

Berry — The quality of ripe, sweet fruit in certain red wines, notably younger merlot and cabernet sauvignon.

Big — A description used for concentrated, rich, full-flavored wines. It's a compliment.

Blanc de blanc — White from white, meaning a sparkling wine made only from chardonnay rather than a blend of chardonnay and pinot noir.

Blanc de noir — Or, white wine from red grapes, often used for sparkling wines made with pinot noir. The skins of the grapes are removed before they color the wine.

Blanc fume — Wine made with the sauvignon blanc grape. Also called fume blanc.

Blending — Combining grape varieties or wines to make one wine that's greater than its parts.

Blush — A pale, rose-shaded wine that's made with red grapes.

Body — The texture, alcoholic content, and mouth feel of the wine, whether full, medium or light. It's tactile. Consider the range between skim milk and heavy cream.

Botrytis cinerea — A mold that concentrates the sugar and flavor in the grape, often yielding outstanding dessert wines. It's also called "noble rot." All rot on grapes isn't.

Bouquet — The scents that arise from fermentation and aging in the barrel and the bottle. The combination of the alcohol and acids in the wine come together in fermentation and aging in the bottle to form the bouquet, which typically may be a floral, fruity, or earthy. Complex bouquets develop in aging.

Breathe — Aeration. After the cork is removed and the wine is exposed to air, it starts to breathe. Better reds benefit from it. Sparkling wine goes flat.

Briary — Often used to describe red wines with bite, tannin and some spiciness. Zinfandels frequently earn the description.

Brix — The scale for measuring sugar content in grapes and wine, and the last name of the scientist who invented it.

Brut — Designation for the driest Champagnes and sparkling wines. Drier than "extra dry."

Bung — The plug used to seal the wine barrel. Of course, it goes into a bung hole.

Buttery — The scent and sometimes the taste of melted butter, invariably associated with rich chardonnays. It's a positive trait.

Canopy — The leaves and shoots of the grapevine.

Cap — The skin, seeds and stems that rise to the top of the juice during fermentation.

Cassis — The flavor of black currants, usually a reference point in describing cabernet sauvignon.

Chaptalization — The addition of sugar to the fermentation vat. Used to produce alcohol when grapes are underripe.

Chateau — In wineworld, used when referring to a vineyard or an estate. They're not all castles.

Chewy — Mouth-filling wines that are rich and intense. If not quite chewable, they still give the impression.

Citrus — As in grapefruit and lemon. Some white wines have citrus-like aroma and flavor.

Clone — A plant reproduced by graftings or cuttings to duplicate qualities of the original.

Closed — Refers to a young wine yet to show its potential.

Crisp — The presence of

refreshing, balanced acidity in a wine. Appealing in certain white wines.

Complex — A balanced wine with levels of flavor; depth, distinctions, subtleties.

Cru — French, meaning "growth," used as part of a vineyard's ranking in quality.

Crushing — Getting the juice out of the grape, typically with a crusher-stemmer. Grapes are broken and the juice, skin and seeds are separated from leaves and stems. Juice for white wine is separated from skins and seeds. To make red wine, the juice, skins and seeds go into the tanks together for fermentation.

Disgorgement — Removal of sediment from bottles of sparkling wine. The sediment that has settled around the cork, because of its upside down positioning and regular turning by staff, is in the neck of the bottle. The neck is put in a solution to freeze the sediment, which exits when the cork is removed.

Dry — A wine that isn't sweet.

Dumb — A wine that's closed. It happens months after bottling and can last a long time.

Enology — The study of wine-making.

Esters — Compounds produced during fermentation and aging. They add complexity to the wine.

Fat — Used to describe a rich wine that doesn't overdo the acid.

Fermentation — How grape juice becomes wine. When yeast from the grapes or added by the winemaker triggers the process of turning sugar to alcohol. Fermentation takes place in small barrels, big vats, stainless steel tanks. Malolactic fermentation converts sharp malic acid to milder lactic acid.

Filtration — A method to clarify wine and get rid of any solids. It can affect flavor in the wine.

Fining — Removing elements that make wines bitter or cloudy.

Finish — What stays on the palate after you've swallowed the wine. It refers to the taste and the texture of the wine. A lingering finish is desirable.

Flabby — Not the same as fat. A flabby wine lacks acidity and flavor. There must be a better word.

Flinty — Used in describing certain dry, white wines, which have a mineral aroma and taste suggesting flint. This does stretch the vocabulary.

Floral — Wines that have a hint of flowers in the aroma. Typically in white wines such as gewürztraminer and riesling.

Fortified — Describes wines to which neutral spirits or

brandy have been added to increase the alcohol content. Port and Sherry, Madeira and Marsala are some fortified wines.

Forward — A wine that has matured early.

Foxy — Typically used describing the aroma and taste of wines made from hybrid grapes in the northeastern United States. They have an intensely grapey, musky character.

Free-run — The juice that flows before any pressure is applied to the grapes.

Fresh — Young, lively.

Fruity — It refers to the taste of the fruit from the grapes in the wine. A wine becomes less fruity as it ages.

Grafting — Attaching the bud shoot to the rootstock of grapevines.

Grapey — When a wine suggests the qualities of raw grapes.

Grassy — The scent of freshly cut grass, usually used describing sauvignon blanc.

Gravelly — An earthy aroma.

Green — Wine from under-ripe grapes.

Hard — A very tannic or acidic wine. As in hard to drink.

Horizontal tasting — A tasting of wines from the same vintage but from different producers.

Hot — A wine with too much alcohol.

Ice wine — Dessert wine made with grapes frozen on the vine or commercially. The juice is concentrated, intense, with plenty of sugar and acid.

Lean — A wine that's short on fruit.

Leathery — Applied to tannic red wines that have a smell similar to leather, largely because of the the wooden barrels in which they mature.

Lees — The sediment at the barrel's bottom after the wine has been pumped out. Wines sometimes are left "on the lees" to gain flavor.

Legs — Those rivulets that go down the side of the glass after you've swirled the wine. Yes, they suggest the body of the wine.

Limpid — A clear, bright wine.

Lush — A very drinkable wine that's rich and fruity.

Maceration — The time grape juice remains in contact with skins and seeds.

Mouth-filling — Used to describe wines that seem to coat the mouth with flavors and textures.

Must — Crushed white grapes and juice after pressing; red grape juice with the skin, seeds and pulp after the

crush and before fermentation.

Nose — The bouquet of fruity and flowery aromas in a wine.

Oaky — The term stems from wines that are aged in white oak barrels, made from wood in Europe and the U.S. New oak barrels contribute toasty flavor and aroma to the wine. Traces of vanilla also may stem from oak. In some wines, oak becomes a dominant and not very beneficial factor; the wine is "overoaked." Red wines and chardonnays often are aged in oak.

Off dry — Slight sweetness.

Open — A ready-to-drink wine.

Oxidation — Deterioration due to air exposure. The wine basically goes stale.

Phylloxera — A parasite that weakens the grapevine's roots. *Vitis vinifera* is very vulnerable, so these vines have been grafted onto native American rootstocks generally resistant to this plant louse.

Plonk — British slang for poor wine.

Pourriture noble — French term for *botrytis cinerea*.

Pruning — Cutting undesirable old growth to shape the vine for the most efficiency.

Punt — That indentation at the bottom of many wine bottles.

Racking — Transferring juice from tank to tank, or barrel to barrel, leaving behind the sediment. Not always a torturous process.

Residual sugar — Grape sugar unfermented or reintroduced to the wine.

Rootstock — The lower part of the root and buds used to reproduce the plant.

Round — A harmonious, graceful, balanced, full-bodied wine.

Sediment — Those deposits at the bottom of the wine bottle. Mainly with red wines as they age and tannins and pigments separate. White-wine sediment is almost colorless.

Soft — Refers to a fruity, easy-on-the-palate wine with comparatively low acid and tannin. In some wines, it's an attractive quality, but it also may suggest lack of balance. Used too much.

Sparkling wine — Wine with carbon dioxide bubbles. The carbon dioxide is either produced naturally or added. The style is perfected in Champagne.

Spicy — When a wine has the characteristics of spices, such as pepper or cinnamon. This may be from the oak of the barrel, or the grape variety. It doesn't necessarily suggest heat.

Steely — Lean and acidic, but well-balanced. Applies generally to white wines.

Still wine — Wine without carbon dioxide bubbles.

Sulfites — You see "contains sulfites" on wine labels. These are salts, from sulfurous acid. The information is on the label to state that sulfur dioxide entered into the winemaking. Some have allergies to sulfites. For most, no source of concern.

Table wine — A still, unfortified wine.

Tannin — Tannins are compounds that act as preservatives and give wine a longer life. They come from the skins, stems and seeds, and give the wine structure. They're astringent and result in a puckery quality early on. Tannins soften during the aging process.

Tight — When a young wine is underdeveloped, it's tight.

Toasty — As in toasted bread. Wines kept in oak barrels with toasted interiors have this quality. It's most evident in chardonnays and in certain sparkling wines.

Ullage — When wine evaporates, space opens in the bottle or the barrel and causes exposure to air. That space is ullage. Winemakers minimize ullage by adding wine.

Varietal — A wine that uses its primary grape as its name. Varietal character means what a specific grape brings to the wine. You won't mistake cabernet sauvignon and gamay, chardonnay and gewürztraminer.

Vegetal — As in vegetables. Some wines do have suggestions of, for example, bell peppers. If there's too much of this quality, the wine isn't very good.

Velvety — Smooth.

Vertical tasting — A tasting of wines from the same winery but from different years.

Viniculture — Winemaking science.

Vintage — The year of the grape harvest from which the wine is made. Nonvintage wines used the grapes from more than one year.

Viticulture — The study of grapes and cultivating grapevines.

Vitis labrusca — A North American species of vines, primarily from the northeastern United States and Canada. Concord and catawba are from this species.

Vitis riparia — Also an American species of vines, used for rootstocks that resist phylloxera. Baco noir is from this species.

Vitis vinifera — The species of native European vines that yields the classic wines, from chardonnay and riesling to cabernet sauvignon and pinot noir. There are thousands of grapes in this species, which is planted worldwide and produces almost all the wine you drink.

CHAPTER 10

What to Buy Now

The vintages revisited

The grapevine tells a vintage story. In any year, it can be part comedy and part thriller. Or, depending on the weather, a tale of terror. And when all goes right: a classic.

The term "vintage" is from the French "vendage," or harvest. It refers to the year that the grapes are harvested, and to the wines made from those grapes.

In the United States, for a wine to be designated with a vintage, 95 per cent or more of the grapes used must have been harvested in that year. When grapes from more than one year go into a wine and no single harvest accounts for at least 95 percent of the content, it's a non-vintage wine.

Wine used to be kept in barrels instead of bottles. It wasn't until the late 1700s, when bottles were produced in roughly the shapes they are today, that extensive vintage dating began. Since the size and quality of the grape harvest can vary significantly from year to year in regions from Bordeaux and Burgundy to the North Fork and the Hamptons, it's wise to note the vintage at least as a shorthand way of judging likely quality.

But assessments of wines typically are made extremely early. Often it's only after blending that the evolving wine can be savored.

Before that, you could say all wines are vintage wines. Blending of grapes from different years is a common practice, especially when a winemaker wants to ensure that a particular wine is the same year after year.

So, consider the vintage a guide, suggesting which wines should be consumed now and which ones will mature in the cellar or stick around well in the hall closet.

That said, non-vintage wines often are fine, too, bringing together more than one year's grapes to achieve a better overall result. Just because a wine is vintage-dated doesn't mean it's a better wine.

What matters more than the year is the bottle's content. From what's deemed an excellent vintage, you may find wines in a very broad range.

On the North Fork and in the Hamptons, vintages have been quite good during the 1990s. About half of the decade's vintages have produced recommended wines from almost every winery.

Because Long Island's wine industry is comparatively young, it's difficult to gauge the lifespan of many of the region's wines. But based on recent tastings, you could go back as far as 1988 and enjoy mature, elegant red wines.

White wines dating to 1993 continue to be sound choices, with a few from earlier in the decade very drinkable, too. And some sparkling and fortified wines from 1991 and 1992 have aged well.

Following is a brief guide to Long Island vintages since the mid-1980s. Most of the wines from the early 1980s are no longer available. You still may be able to find some reds produced from 1985 to 1988. But the Long Island wine on the market today is dominated by the years from 1993 through 1997, with certain 1991 and 1992 wines completing the rack.

1997

Local winemakers are talking about the 1997 vintage with a reverence typically reserved for the '27 Yankees. The harvest was about two weeks later than usual thanks to so much sun after Labor Day. There were drought conditions in summer. Flavors were concentrated.

1996

A much lighter style of wine compared with the winners of the previous three years. Cool and rainy weather meant vineyards had to pick the grapes as late as possible. The fruit wasn't as ripe. So far, the whites are better than the reds. Average overall.

1995

Lots of summer heat and warm, dry fall weather boosted the grapes. It was a big crop as well as an outstanding one. This is a vintage to seek, with uniformly first-rate wines. Some of the reserve reds and deluxe blends have yet to be released. They should be a treat.

1994

The summer was warm, but the heat didn't last into September. A very good vintage, with similarities to 1993 and 1995, and many appealing wines. In some cases, the wines were better than the '93s. But for most wineries, this year was a slight dip between two peaks.

1993

For consistency and quality, the best vintage since 1988, whether for reds or whites. The hot, dry summer wasn't overtaken by early September rains. Top levels of sugar and acid at harvest, which took place a couple of weeks earlier than usual because the grapes ripened so well in the consistent sunshine. The yields were lower than normal: terrific wine, but not enough of it.

1992

The summer was cool, and the ripening of the grapes was delayed, in some cases more than a month. But the result was better than expected. Yields were high. The wines, satisfactory.

1991

Hurricane Bob made a dramatic cameo appearance. But the summer storm hit Long Island while the berries on the vines were hard. The fruit was fine and the yield good. So were a lot of the wines.

1990

The growing season was hot and wet. Autumn: warm and drier. A cold snap the previous fall didn't help, either. The yield was fairly small, due to weather and hungry birds. But some wines were very good.

1989

Wet and cool. Winemakers wince when this hard year is discussed, especially after '88's pleasures.

1988

The breakthrough vintage, with among the region's richest red wines, from cabernet sauvignon to merlot, which are drinking well today. The season was long, hot and dry. Excellent, ripe fruit.

1987

Rainy late in the season and forgettable.

1986

The dry and hot season produced serviceable to very good wines, especially white wines, depending on the producer. Few remain.

1985

Hurricane Gloria. The surviving grapes yielded modest wines.

Some Good Choices

Each winery has its specialties. Here are some of the wines that will give you representative tastes. I've listed good buys, top wines (the highlights), and when applicable, something particularly distinctive, different and worth a try: Call it serendipity.

Banfi Old Brookville Vineyards
Highlight: 1996 Chardonnay

Bedell Cellars
Highlight: 1994 Merlot Reserve
Best buy: 1995 Merlot
Serendipity: EIS dessert wine

Bidwell Vineyards
Highlight: 1996 Sauvignon Blanc
Best buy: 1995 Dry White Riesling

Channing Daughters Winery
Highlight: 1996 Brick Kiln Chardonnay

Corey Creek Vineyards
Highlight: 1995 Reserve Chardonnay
Best buy: 1995 Chardonnay
Serendipity: 1997 Rosé

Duck Walk Vineyards
Highlight: 1995 Chardonnay Reserve
Best buy: Southampton White
Serendipity: 1995 Aphrodite

Gristina Vineyards
Highlight: 1994 Andy's Field Merlot
Best buy: 1997 Rosé of Cabernet Sauvignon
Serendipity: 1995 Andy's Field Chardonnay

Hargrave Vineyard
Highlight: 1995 Pinot Noir
Best buy: 1996 Chardonette
Serendipity: 1993 QED cabernet blend

Jamesport Vineyards
Highlight: Grand Cuvée
Best buy: 1996 Sauvignon Blanc
Serendipity: 1995 Late Harvest Riesling

Laurel Lake Vineyards
Highlight: 1995 Chardonnay

The Lenz Winery
Highlight: 1994 Estate Bottled Merlot
Best buy: 1994 Vineyard Selection Chardonnay
Serendipity: 1993 Cuvée

Loughlin Vineyards
Highlight: 1995 Chardonnay

Macari Vineyards
Highlight: 1996 Barrel Fermented Chardonnay
Best buy: 1997 Sauvignon Blanc
Serendipity: 1997 Rosé d'une Nuit

Osprey's Dominion Winery
Highlight: 1996 Reserve Chardonnay
Best buy: 1995 Chardonnay
Serendipity: 1996 Pinot Noir

Palmer Vineyards
Highlight: 1995 Merlot Reserve
Best buy: 1996 Pinot Blanc
Serendipity: 1995 Select Late Harvest Gewürztraminer

Paumanok Vineyards
Highlight: 1995 Tuthills Lane Cabernet Sauvignon
Best buy: 1997 Chenin Blanc
Serendipity: 1997 Late Harvest Sauvignon Blanc

Peconic Bay Vineyards
Highlight: 1995 Epic Acre Merlot
Best buy: 1995 White Riesling
Serendipity: 1994 Select Late Harvest Riesling

Pellegrini Vineyards
Highlight: 1994 Vintner's Pride Encore
Best buy: 1995 Chardonnay
Serendipity: 1996 Finale

Pindar Vineyards
Highlight: 1995 Mythology
Best buy: 1996 Gamay Beaujolais
Serendipity: 1995 Cabernet Port

Pugliese Vineyards
Highlight: 1993 Blanc de Blanc
Best buy: Red Table Wine
Serendipity: 1995 Sparkling Merlot

Sagpond/Wolffer Vineyards
Highlight: 1995 Estate Selection Merlot
Best buy: 1996 Rosé
Serendipity: 1995 Pinot Noir

Schneider Vineyards
Highlight: 1995 Cabernet Franc

Ternhaven Cellars
Highlight: 1995 Merlot ✦

ABOUT THE AUTHOR

Peter M. Gianotti is Newsday's restaurant and wine critic. Before he started reviewing restaurants, Gianotti was a Washington correspondent, economics writer, book critic and New York City reporter. He is the author of "Dining Out with Newsday," 1997 and 1998 editions. He is co-author of Newsday's "Long Island Restaurant Guide," and "Eats NYC." Gianotti received his master's degree from Columbia University, where he also was a Bagehot Fellow, and his bachelor's degree from Fordham University, where he has taught journalism. He was born in Brooklyn, raised in Queens, and lives on Long Island.

Editor
Phyllis Singer

Director of Editorial Design
Bob Eisner

Art Director
Joe Toscano

Coordinating Editor
Jack Millrod

Copy Editor
James R. Stear

Marketing Manager
MeiPu Yang

Production Coordinator
Julian Stein